THE
THOUGHT
IMPOSSIBLE

JOAN GIESON

DEDICATION

I dedicate this book to God and my family.

ACKNOWLEDGMENTS

Tutz and Dot Palermo
My mom and dad who gave me life, raised me as a God-fearing, strong woman and taught me the gift of love, that I share with everyone I meet. I owe everything to both of them for my life as it is today. I love you!

Frank Gieson
My precious husband who stands with me as we have shared life together through the ups and downs and in between. Neither of us could have done it alone. I love you.

Mike, Kim, Tom, Joanie, and Anthony
My beautiful children and grandchildren. You are the sunshine in my heart and life, I depend on all of you for love, strength, help, courage, and answers. You are my everything. I love you more than words can describe. I hope you know that.

Kathryn Kuhlman and Benny Hinn
*W*hat a privilege to serve in both of the greatest ministries of my time. It has been a tremendous honor and blessing for me and my family. Thank you, Father, for calling me.

To my precious Friends
*R*oxAnne Olson, Cheryl Green, Kevin Banks, Professor Joe Novak, Bill McKee, and many more. You send me gifts, take care of me, pray for me, lift up my arms. I love you very much. You make it possible for me to pray for the thousands. Joe and Gwen Frey—you have made a 40-year-old dream come true. Thank you God for sending each one of them into my life.

CONTENTS

INTRODUCTION

*L*et's face it. I am probably the most unlikely of all people to be doing what I do. I don't fit the normal category. I am not a theologian or a medical doctor. But God has allowed me the incredible honor to both witness and participate in the largest miracle ministries of our time.

For the last decade of Kathryn Kuhlman's life, the Lord gave me the awesome privilege of working closely with her—heading up her Midwest office in St. Louis, Missouri, and being part of Ms. Kuhlman's ministry team across the nation.

A double portion was poured out on me when Benny Hinn asked me to join his international crusade staff, which I have now been part of for many years. If you watch his television ministry, you have seen me bring to the platform and introduce hundreds of people who have received their miracle.

In addition, we just celebrated the 50th anniversary of the Gieson's Annual Christmas Outreach in St. Louis. Every year we feed and give special gifts to thousands of needy families. It has grown into one of the largest ministries of its kind in the nation.

What you are about to read are true accounts of the amazing hand of God at work. I have personally seen enough miracles to fill countless books, but I have chosen these particular stories to build your faith, enlarge your vision, and help you receive what God has in store for you.

On these pages I want to share:

- How an anointed prayer ended a plague of sickness in our son.
- The story of an epileptic who broke free from his wheelchair.
- How the aroma of God's Spirit brought healing and deliverance.
- The account of a little girl who was dying of cancer and how she was able to give her daddy the best birthday present ever.
- How a leading educator with a chronic heart condition was instantly made whole.
- The story of how an amazing surge of life entered a woman who had died on a city street.
- The documented report of how God miraculously multiplied food for the hungry and needy.
- What happened when our daughter's honeymoon plans turned into a nightmare.
- The chance meeting in an Italian restaurant that brought reconciliation to an entire family.
- How a young woman who was declared legally blind suddenly received her sight.
- The journey of a boy with autism and no hope who became an honor graduate.
- The account of a woman who experienced not one, but *five* miracles
  —and so much more.

I pray that as you read this book you will begin to believe, as never before, for *Things Thought Impossible.*

— *Joan Gieson*

One

A MIRACLE FOR MICHAEL

*Is anyone among you sick? Let him call
for the elders of the church, and let them pray
over him, anointing him with oil in the name of
the Lord. And the prayer of faith will save the
sick, and the Lord will raise him up.*

– JAMES 5:14-15

*A*s I mentioned earlier, our first child was a son who we named Michael.

I was in labor with him for one week, but every time I rushed to the hospital I was told it still wasn't time and they would send me home again.

On Halloween night, 1959, I just knew this was it and the hospital finally agreed. They placed me in a room at the end of the hall with another young woman.

We each were given a bracelet with a sponge inside that was filled with ether. The nurse told us, "If you have a major pain, take a whiff and it will help you get through the discomfort."

They raised the sides of the beds and warned us not to get up by ourselves or we might fall. "If you need help just press the call button and we'll be right there." I was whiffing on that bracelet whenever I even *thought* I was going to have a pain—and before long I was feeling a little loopy. Needing to use the restroom, I pushed the call button but no one responded. So I climbed over the side rails and went into the bathroom by myself. The two of us were so goofy from the ether we had no idea what we were really doing. I'm sure the nurses were exasperated with us.

This was a time when husbands were not permitted in the delivery rooms. They had to stay in a special waiting area until the baby was born; then they would be called.

New fathers were allowed to see their baby through the nursery window after they were all cleaned up and sleeping like little angels. After many hours of screaming and pushing, Mike popped out—and all our lives changed.

I wanted to nurse Mike and they gave me instructions how to do this, but when they brought the little guy to me I was so exhausted from a week of false labor and then real labor, not to mention the ether, I was out of it. My new son cried a lot and I simply didn't know what to do.

It was as if someone had just dropped this baby in my arms and said, "Your motherly instincts will kick in." No way! I was an emotional wreck. Far too soon for my thinking, the doctor said I was being discharged.

PLAGUED WITH SICKNESS

I had planned forever to be the best mom in the history of the world, but already I hit some major roadblocks. I went to my mom's house with my husband and Mike. She kindly offered to help me for a couple of weeks—and I thought I could learn everything I needed to know during that time.

About three days later, Michael developed a bad cough, so I immediately took him to a pediatrician, who told me he needed antibiotics and gave him a shot. I wasn't too happy, but he was the doctor.

From that day forward, Mike's childhood was plagued with sickness. He had many allergies and always seemed to have the croup. We kept a vaporizer running in his room and he was constantly on medicine.

By the time he was seven years old, Michael had caught pneumonia about nine times.

FRIGHTENED BEYOND WORDS

During these years, Frank and I had become born again Christians and we were trusting God to heal our son. He had been sick often, but this time it seemed worse than ever. He was taking shots for allergies and pills for asthma, but this bout seemed different. He had a raging fever of 104 degrees. I was frightened beyond words.

The doctor came to our house to see him, but he didn't want Mike to go into the hospital. The reason being that each time he went, he would pick up whatever was going around.

The physician said, "He has pneumonia in both lungs and you need to be with him constantly." This was in case he could not breathe, at which time I was to call for an ambulance immediately so they could administer oxygen.

I gave him aspirin to try and bring his fever down, but that did not work. I put him in tepid bath water, but that had no affect either.

Through all of this, Michael was a little trooper. He would read his school books, draw pictures and play for hours with his dog, Joey.

CALLING FOR AN ELDER

Desperate to help our son, I phoned my friend Annie, the woman who had led me to the Lord, and began to cry when I told her how Michael was suffering.

"Annie," I sobbed, "I read in the Bible about the elders of the church praying for the sick and they would recover. Since your husband, Chuck, is an elder of our church, would he please come over with anointing oil and pray over Mike?"

"I'll certainly ask him," she responded.

A little later, she called back to tell me, "No, my husband doesn't really believe that laying hands on the sick is for today. He says those times are gone."

I was stunned. Even as a new Christian, I believed that whatever the Bible said was true—and healing was not only for the times of Jesus and the disciples, but for us today. As far as I was concerned there was no discussion or question on the topic.

So I called her back and *insisted* that her husband come over. He was a precious man whom I respected greatly.

About an hour later he returned my call and told me he was on his way with some olive oil. I had no idea why he had such a sudden change of heart, but I knew the Lord was at work.

I went to Mike's bedroom and explained that an elder from our church was coming over to pray for him to get better. That was okay with him.

Shortly, Chuck was at our door and we were so pleased to see him. I took him to our son's room and he said, "Mike, I am going to place some oil on the front of your head and pray that you will be healed."

Mike replied, "Yes, sir. I believe when you do that I will be well."

Then Chuck read James 5:14-15: *"Is anyone among you sick? Let him call for the elders of the church, and let them pray over him, anointing him with oil in the name of the Lord. And the prayer of faith will save the sick, and the Lord will raise him up."*

The elder opened the bottle of oil, touched Mike's forehead with a few drops and prayed. Within 30 minutes, our son was completely made whole.

Today, he is in his 50s and has never had a reoccurring attack of pneumonia or asthma.

AN INSPIRATION TO MIKE

From that experience forward, Chuck and Annie began praying for the sick and God honored their faith with many, many miracles. Scores of people heard the Gospel in their home, and they would share Christ wherever they went—whether it be at a restaurant or a shopping center. All their children and grandchildren are born again Christians and serve the Lord.

Because of their witness, by the time Mike was eight years old he was begging me to let him go to the mall near our home and hand out Gospel tracts.

Later, in the mid-70s, when Kathryn Kuhlman came to St. Louis for Miracle Services, I was asked to head her foundation office in the mid-west,

Over the years, we chartered over 200 buses to bring people to her services in Pittsburgh and other cities.

As a teenager, Michael was in charge of helping sick people get on and off the buses. If they were in wheelchairs, he made sure they were settled inside the auditorium. He assisted them when the needed to use the restroom—a task a teen wouldn't normally volunteer to do.

--------------------------------◦◦◦--------------------------------

He and his sister loved Ms. Kuhlman,
and she loved them in return.

OH, WHAT WE HAD LEARNED

I can still remember the day we received a phone call in 1976 from Gene Martin telling us that Ms. Kuhlman had been called home to be with Jesus. Mike took the news very hard. "Mom," he cried, "we will never see another miracle as long as we live."

I was in tears too, but the Holy Spirit checked me with these words: "If that was all her life was worth, it was worth nothing."

I couldn't understand for a moment, but then I realized what He was saying to me. If what she knew and the gift of miracles He had given her had died with her, it was all for naught.

I told Michael, "There was much more to Ms. Kuhlman than miracles. She taught us the Word of God and mentored us in everything she did. She told us how important it was to read His Word everyday—to talk to Him and never to make a move until He directed us. She instructed us regarding how to hear from our heavenly Father, how to give to others, and to die to ourselves."

Then I continued, "Ms. Kuhlman taught us how to forgive and receive forgiveness, how to trust God with everything in our lives, and let our words be trustworthy."

After our talk, he never again cried over it. From that day on, we remembered her wisdom and guidance. even though she was no longer here to teach us. We felt thankful to know such a person who pointed us to the Holy Spirit and we realized it was now our turn to teach others what we had experienced.

Michael learned great responsibility from all those years of serving.

As an adult, he became multifaceted, working in fields of catering, land planning, and as a businessman greatly respected in St. Louis. Yet, he has never departed from the teachings he learned so many years ago.

He has taken "little faith" and built it into "great faith." This is what the Lord expects of His children.

Two

"Joan, Joan. Find That Noise!"

Every good gift and every perfect gift is from above, and comes down from the Father of lights, with whom there is no variation or shadow of turning.

– JAMES 1:17

I was standing backstage during one of Kathryn Kuhlman's services, when I heard her say, "Joan, Joan, find that noise. Find that noise!"

It was a sound I'd never heard before—like electricity skipping across a wire in a lightning storm; *cssh, cssh, cssh, cssh, cssh, cssh."*

I quickly looked to my right and there was a young man standing there. He was one of the ushers who had volunteered for the crusade.

His name was Bill Banks, a phenomenal person who had been healed of terminal cancer. He radiated the presence of God and the healing experience he had gone through. Given only 48 hours to live, as people prayed, God pulled him back from the brink of death.

16

I said to Bill, "Will you please go with me? Let's find the noise Ms. Kuhlman is talking about." As I mentioned earlier, she didn't like any distractions in her services—no moving about, no children crying.

We ran from behind the stage, all the way around the perimeter of the auditorium. Then, suddenly, it felt as if we were being drawn to an area where those in wheelchairs were located. Like a magnet, something kept pulling us until we came to a spot where we couldn't go any further. It was as if a big wall was there and we couldn't penetrate it.

I said to Bill, "There it is—over there!"

It sounded like it was generating from the other side of the building. Everyone could hear it—the grating noise made your hair stand up on the back of your neck.

All of a sudden I saw a commotion going on in the wheelchair section. It centered on a young man I had noticed hours before the service began.

Bill and I walked up to about six feet behind the wheelchair, but could go no closer. We couldn't talk to him or touch him. We just stood there and watched the disturbance surrounding this person.

A PIERCING SOUND

The Kiel Auditorium in St. Louis held about 17,000 and there wasn't an empty seat in the house. Thousands had been turned away.

But now, every eye in the building, from the ground floor to the rafters, was focused on this man.

Earlier, when Kathryn Kuhlman asked, "Joan, Joan, find that noise, find that noise," she held onto the piano as if she needed some stability. The noise was absolutely piercing.

Bill and I watched the young man in his wheelchair. We had gone by him several times prior to the service starting and were concerned. His electric wheelchair had two levers—one allowed him to go forward, and the other backward. When his finger pushed one lever, he would just plow into the people in front of him. Then, he would use his other finger and hit the wheelchairs behind him.

At one point we even thought about asking he and his friends to leave because of the disturbance. Thank God, we didn't.

Accompanying him were a couple of young people they called "Jesus Freaks" during those days. They wore bell bottom blue jeans that were torn at the edges, beads hung around their necks, and bandanas were on their heads. To me, they looked rather grubby. But they were praising God and enjoying every part of the service.

STRAPPED IN

The young man in the wheelchair had a blanket over his lap, but we could see the catheter attached to the side. He wore unattractive red and white striped pants. He was extremely frail and had the body of a boy, but you could tell he was a man.

There was a food tray attached to the front of the wheelchair which held several food items for him to snack on. A cup was strapped to his wrist, and every now and then they would fill it with water—and help him lift it to his lips.

We had no idea of his medical condition, but could see he was extremely spastic and very, very ill. He didn't appear to be able to move any part of his body except the fingers he used to operate the power levers of the wheelchair.

We also noticed that he was strapped in with what looked like thick, government-issued belts. The kind you put around luggage. One was harnessed around his chest and the other right above his hips, both buckled at the back.

Despite his condition, there was no way he was going to get out of that chair or tip it over. Every now and then you would see him tremble. I thought, "If those belts weren't in place, he would catapult right out."

BREAKING FREE

Bill and I were about six feet behind his wheelchair when all of a sudden we heard another sound. It went "Pssshew, Pssshew"—like something breaking. Amazed, we saw the belts that were wrapped around the man, and securely attached in the back, break in the front and come apart. We could hardly believe our eyes. This guy was loose!

The tray was still across the front of his wheelchair, but he started to get up. We saw his hands moving as he was trying to raise himself. In a few seconds he gained a little momentum, and some obvious strength. Then the metal tray crashed to the floor—making a sound that echoed through the whole auditorium.

The young man then rose and stood to his feet. And by this time everyone in the entire building was standing, straining to see what was happening.

We watched as he began to move, and we could tell he could not see. It was also obvious he had not walked for a long time and didn't have his equilibrium. But to everyone's amazement, he took one step, then another, and another, and fumbled his way to the outer aisle of the arena.

Wow! My heart was leaping for joy when he started walking toward the stage. He had pulled the catheter loose from the side of the wheelchair, but it was still attached, dragging behind him.

Bill and I couldn't move a muscle. It was as if we were suspended in space. Even now, it's impossible to fully describe.

I looked up and saw Ms. Kuhlman. This slender woman, dressed in white, had her arms outstretched and was still holding onto the piano for dear life. In the years I served in her ministry, I had never seen her speechless—or at a point where she didn't know what to do. She just watched as this frail figure came toward her.

By the time he reached the stage, you could see his momentum increase and his balance improve. His legs now had strength, but his sight and direction seemed guided by sound.

He placed his hands on the edge of the stage and, like a young man leaping over a fence, he jumped up on the platform.

Everyone was thinking, "Who is this person? What is he going to do?" All we could do was watch.

FALLING FROM THE SKY

He walked up to Ms. Kuhlman and said, "I'll be right back. I'll be right back." Then he turned around, walked back to the edge of the stage, jumped off, and went back to his wheelchair.

Next, he began fooling around with some wires that were hooked up to the battery and pulled the battery out of its casing. He took off once again and placed the battery on top of the stage and jumped back up.

As he made his way forward, we heard a third noise. First, there was what sounded like electricity skipping across a wire in a storm. The second was when the belts broke loose. Now the third—which was the congregation in an audible "whuooo" that resounded through the auditorium.

We were amazed as we watched the almighty power of God come alive before our very eyes. It was awe inspiring.

"Ms. Kuhlman," he exclaimed, holding the battery in his hands, "I couldn't do this before."

"Well," she told him, "put the thing down."

He followed her instructions and she asked, "What's happening to you, young man."

"My name is Bill Spears," he began. I am from House Springs, Missouri"—which is about two hours from St. Louis. "And I am 300 percent disabled."

"How can that be?" she asked.

The young man continued, "I was in the United States Air Force and parachuted out of a plane." He told how something went horribly wrong and when he landed he was seriously injured. From that point on he had suffered with grand mal seizures—epilepsy. As he was trying to recover from his injuries, they diagnosed him with multiple sclerosis. Sadly, he then lost his sight. So there were three separate 100 percent disabilities.

"I've been laying in a bed that has a pulsating mattress 24/7," he explained. "I never get out of bed, and am rarely without oxygen to help me breathe. The doctors have to come to my home."

Evidently, the mattress was one that had rollers inside which circulated from one place to another so it would move his flesh around, preventing bedsores.

He told how they put a hospital bed in the sunroom of his home so he could see the outside light, "But all I could make out were blurry images." He couldn't read, and only listened to audio books or to the soundtracks of movies.

"I've been in this condition for years," he told Ms. Kuhlman. "The doctors have given up and said there's nothing more they can do for me."

"How did you get here?" Ms. Kuhlman asked.

"Friends brought me," he responded.

WAS IT TRUE?

What we had witnessed was an absolute miracle!

When the service was over and the crowd dispersed, Frank and I walked to the top deck of the parking lot and couldn't stop talking about what had taken place. We looked down, and there was this young man and the people who brought him, walking across the street. He was pushing his own wheelchair!

Frank turned to me and said, "I'm not sure about this guy. I think I'll do some investigation so the ministry is 100 percent sure of his healing."

I was ready to take what happened at face value, but Frank is cautious about such things.

We remembered that he told Ms. Kuhlman on stage the name of his hometown.

NO TIME TO REST

Protecting the evangelist's reputation and ministry was more than a passing thought. After all, Frank and I had been asked to run her ministry office in the Midwest from St. Louis. We had to book the auditoriums, rent the pianos and organs, handle the advertising, and answer the thousands of phone calls pertaining to her services.

We also scheduled the usher training meetings and choir rehearsals with her long time musical director, Dr. Arthur Metcalfe. In St. Louis, the largest Presbyterian church in the area let us use their facilities for these events.

It was quite an operation. People called from all over the world with interpreters on the phone. They had heard about the miracles and were making arrangements for their desperately ill loved ones.

It was just Frank, myself, and a secretary. We were booking hotel rooms for people, finding transportation for them, and so much more.

As you can imagine, at the conclusion of one of these meetings we were all exhausted.

At the end of this particular service, Ms. Kuhlman announced, "In just a few days, I'm going to be in Las Vegas Nevada. We are going to have a great Miracle Service there."

Then, to our surprise, she said, "Joan and Frank will bring you to Las Vegas. Just call them and they will make the arrangements for you. They will charter a bus or a plane."

Oh, my goodness! We thought we would have a little rest for a few days with no phone calls, but this was not the way it was going to be.

THE DOCTOR NEARLY FAINTED

As we were standing on the parking deck, watching the young man who had just been so magnificently healed, Frank gave his word of caution.

"Joan, I'm going to find out who his doctor is, because he told us from the platform that the physicians came to his home."

We had very little sleep that night—excited about hearing Ms. Kuhlman saying we were going to be with her in Las Vegas.

The next afternoon, Frank called an operator and asked for the numbers of some physicians in the area of House Springs, Missouri.

After a couple of no-answer calls, he finally reached a doctor's office. "Hello, my name is Frank Gieson," he began. "We have just met a man who said he was having home visits from a doctor in House Springs. We want to know if your office has treated Bill Spears."

"Oh, my goodness," replied the nurse. "Do you know Bill Spears?"

"Yes," Frank answered. "We just met him last night."

She replied. "He came here this morning—and he's had a miracle!"

The nurse explained how the doctor had always gone to Bill's home, "But when he walked in, the doctor nearly fainted. He couldn't believe what he was seeing."

She told Frank how Bill had gained an incredible amount of weight. When he walked in, the doctor yelled, "Bill, is that really you?" They put him on the scales and he had gained over 50 pounds. Incredible! The red and white striped pants no longer fit. He was wearing clothes he hadn't worn for a long, long time.

Bill was explaining to the doctor, "I received a miracle— and I'm a different person."

After a full examination the physician concluded there was absolutely nothing wrong with him.

A Documented Miracle

When we heard this our heads were spinning with happiness. The nurse said, "All we know is that Bill Spears was a very ill patient, and now he is healthy. He was blind and now he can see. He could not walk, had multiple sclerosis and grand mal seizures, and now he appears to be absolutely normal."

Frank and I were finally able to talk with the doctor and asked if he would send us a letter verifying everything he had told us—and he did.

What a day it was. The doctor didn't know what had really taken place. He had never heard of Kathryn Kuhlman or a miracle service. We tried to explain the best we could.

"SOLD OUT"

At our office, the telephone started ringing and didn't stop. Every call was about someone wanting to go to Las Vegas, to the great miracle service. Kathryn Kuhlman had never been there before and people were excited that a mighty woman of God was going to what is called "Sin City."

When you think about it, this was just the kind of place where Jesus would go.

Time was short, and when I began calling hotels for reservations, I was hearing, "No Ma'am. We're sold out. We don't have any rooms available."

I learned there were "junkets" available for gamblers, but that's not what we were going for.

When I phoned the airlines, it was too short of notice to charter a plane, "But we can book your people on regularly scheduled flights."

Immediately, we began making reservations for people on one particular TWA flight that had seats available. However, I knew many more would be calling to go.

I also felt that those traveling such a distance might want to see the area—including Hoover Dam and Lake Mead. So I arranged for a charter bus to meet the plane, take us to our hotel (if we ever found one) and be at our disposal.

We called and called for accommodations, but nothing. I remember sitting at my desk, crying, "Jesus, You've got to help us. We can't possibly go until we have some rooms."

I decided to make one more call—to a Las Vegas tourist bureau that supposedly could make all kinds of arrangements. When I phoned the receptionist said, "Let me give you a number. I'm sure they can accommodate you."

Quickly, I dialed and explained, "I need thirty rooms"—telling them we were coming to Vegas for a miracle service at the auditorium with Kathryn Kuhlman.

"Yes, Mrs. Gieson. We can help you."

I was shocked, and answered, "You can?" It was the Marina Hotel (which has now been absorbed into the MGM Grand).

Once off the phone, I started praising the Lord!

THE REAL STORY

Immediately, I contacted the entire list of those traveling with us. We met at the St. Louis airport and boarded the huge Lockheed L-1011. We occupied the entire middle section.

Seated next to me was Bill Spears—just days after his amazing miracle. He was absolutely charged with the resurrection power of the Son of God that was flowing through his veins. The same power that raised Jesus from the dead, now had gone through Bill. He was alive, yet knew very little about the wonder-working, healing Christ.

Here is what I learned while talking with him. He didn't come to the Kathryn Khulman miracle service because he thought he could be healed or because he believed in Jesus. These "Jesus Freaks" heard about this gravely ill young man in their small town—even though they didn't know him personally. So they said to each other, "Let's see if this fellow will believe enough to get in the car with us and go to the miracle service at Kiel Auditorium."

On arrival at his home, they introduced themselves to his wife and were taken into Bill's bedroom. They told him about the Kathryn Kuhlman meeting (just a couple days away) and that they would really like to take him. "We believe you will be healed," they said in faith.

Bill nodded his head, "Yes."

I also learned that the real reason he wanted get in their car was because he was a smoker, and couldn't light up in his room because of the oxygen tank. So the wheels in his head started churning. He could visualize himself smoking all the way down, while he was there, and all the way back.

These hippie-dressed kids made a pallet for him in their van, hoisted his heavy electric wheelchair in the back and away they went—an hour-plus drive to downtown St. Louis.

He didn't have any idea that these young Christians were being led of God to take him—that he would agree to go—and that he would receiving his healing. But God has His way, whether we realize it or not. He will bring us to the place He wants us to be.

As Hot as Fire

I wish you could have been with us on that plane! Our entire group was gathered around Bill, standing in the aisle, listening to his amazing story. The flight attendants could hardly hand out food and soda because even they wanted to hear about this great miracle of God. Oh, it was exciting!

He gave us the terrifying details of how he jumped out of the plane and was injured and how his condition had deteriorated until he was practically lifeless—just skin and bones. But now his cheeks were full and rosy. You could see how his body had filled out. Bill was even talking about his future: "I want to tell everyone about Jesus."

We asked him, "Bill, how did you get out of the wheelchair? How did you do it?"

He told us that during the service, the wheelchair got as hot as fire, so much so that he could not sit there one second longer. He said. "I had to get out of that thing one way or another or I would have burned up."

It was absolutely marvelous.

"We've Been Waiting for You"

The charter bus was waiting for us and we were rushed to the Marina Hotel. What a gorgeous facility. Big lights flooded the front and there was a bright red carpet in the lobby. We were standing under glistening chandeliers, surrounded by a smiling, smartly dressed staff, eagerly waiting to help us.

I walked to the desk and said, "I'm Joan Gieson and I have brought a group of people from St. Louis.

The receptionist seemed unusually excited. "Ms. Gieson, we've been waiting for you."

I told her, "I smell fresh paint; everything looks like it's brand new."

She replied, "The hotel just opened today, and you are our very first guests."

My mouth dropped. To this day I believe the
Lord arranged this grand opening just for us.

We were their very special guests. In each of our rooms was a beautiful bowl of fruit and fresh flowers. Tucked in the bowl was also a little package tied with a bow. I opened mine and there were gambling chips to be used in their casino. I had to laugh.

We hadn't come to play roulette, blackjack, or to pull the handle of a slot machine. We also weren't there for the food or the shows. We came to praise our God!

PILLS ON THE PLATFORM

The Las Vegas service with Ms. Kuhlman was one of the highlights of her life—and also mine. I will never forget when she called Bill Spears to the platform. He was holding a small wrinkled bag with 20 different prescription pills inside. He put them down and said, "I'll never have to take these again"—and shared the account of his miracle.

His story filled the auditorium with faith and expectation. The presence of the Lord was powerful and God performed mighty works in that unforgettable service.

A few days after we returned to St. Louis, Frank and I went to Bill's house to meet his wife and family. There he was, out in the backyard chopping wood, which he hadn't been able to do for so long. Their home was heated by a wood fireplace.

The miracle that occurred wasn't about him being worthy, holy, or religious. He thought he was doomed—that nothing would ever change and he would die in his wheelchair. But God had another blueprint for his future. One Bill knew nothing about.

A LASTING TESTIMONY

Ms. Kuhlman passed away shortly after her service in Las Vegas. Before she died, she told me that Bill Spears' healing was one of the greatest miracles she had ever seen in her ministry.

I believe his story is one she would have personally written about.

About twenty years later, when I was working with the Benny Hinn crusades, I called Bill Spears and asked if he would go with us to Toronto, Canada, to give his testimony at the Maple Leaf Gardens.

He did, and the account of his healing from God was as powerful as it was the day it happened.

I have been involved in miracle services for decades, and I know that the Lord will do whatever it takes to put you in a position to fulfill what He has purposed for your life.

This very moment, no matter what you are going through, look up to the Master and pray the words of an old hymn:

> *Have thine own way, Lord!*
> *Have thine own way!*
> *Thou art the potter, I am the clay.*
> *Mold me and make me after thy will,*
> *While I am waiting, yielded and still.*

Three

"WHAT IS THAT FRAGRANCE?"

And Jesus went about all Galilee...healing
all kinds of sickness and all kinds of disease among
the people...and they brought to Him all sick people who
were afflicted with various diseases and torments,
and those who were demon-possessed, epileptics,
and paralytics; and He healed them.

– MATTHEW 4:23-24

*W*e serve an amazingly creative God. Just open the door and take a look at the lush green grass, the blue sky, and flowers of every color imaginable. And to think, each human being has a one-of-a-kind fingerprint.

In the years that we were with Kathryn Kuhlman, we organized buses to transport people to the services. Every trip was different; the only thing that remained the same was the bus company itself.

It was exciting to wait by the phone and hear men and woman activate their faith, saying, "I need to go with you on that bus. I am praying for a miracle in my life."

Every need was unique—and some took the trip on behalf of a loved one who was bedridden at home or laid up in the hospital.

I vividly remember one journey we made to Pittsburgh. When those who made reservations gathered in the shopping center parking lot, there were individuals I knew and others I was meeting for the first time.

Just before this particular trip, a good friend called me. His name is Leonard Rebold, a man who found Jesus and had been healed of diabetes. Leonard owned a construction company and was married with four children. He was a frequent passenger—not only to assist me, but to often accompany people who were very sick.

"I THINK THERE'S SOMETHING WRONG"

The night before we left he called, very concerned. "Joan, I have just been in a real estate meeting and there was a lady present who appeared to have some deep personal problems."

He didn't know exactly what was wrong with her, but the well-dressed woman he described was obviously confused and carrying all kinds of burdens. So Leonard told me, "I would really like to bring her on this trip."

I agreed. "Yes, come on. We have two seats left."

So the next morning he and the guest he was praying for showed up. The woman, who was petite and weighed about 105 pounds found a seat in the middle of the bus. But about two hours down the road she began acting rather strange. For example, she got up from her seat and walked up and down the aisle, slapping everyone on the back and behaving very odd.

Immediately, a few people came up to me and expressed their concern: "I am worried. I think there's something wrong with her."

After talking with her, I asked Leonard to keep an eye on his guest. Some of the passengers were getting a bit edgy because of the way she was acting.

Leonard walked back and talked with the women, even praying with her. But she continued her unusual behavior, soon becoming loud and rowdy.

I went to the lady and told her, "Honey, everyone is trying to rest or are praying. If you could just be a little quieter we would appreciate it. If you want to walk up and down the aisle, that's fine. But don't slap anyone on the back. Please, they don't like that."

The woman didn't acknowledge me, yet I knew I spoke clear enough for her to hear.

Sure enough, a few minutes later she started again. This time, her eyes were rolling around in her head. I'd never seen anything like it before. She was acting crazy and I didn't quite know how to handle the situation. At that time I hadn't been a born again believer too long myself.

I called Leonard up to the front and told him, "Please help me with this. I think she has demons."

He confessed, "I thought that last night too, but then she settled down and seemed okay."

WAS IT A DEMON?

I knew from reading scripture that when demons are present, if they are looking for residency they can go into another person.

All I knew to do was to call on the protective blood of Jesus. It covers whatever may be trying to penetrate a life. After all, the Bible tells us that Satan himself must go through the blood of Jesus to get to you (Revelation 12:11). If you are a born again believer, he can't.

I said to Leonard, "We're going to have to do something about this—she's creating too much of a disturbance.

Next, I asked the bus driver to find a safe place and pull over to the side of the road. I had decided to get everybody off the bus so we could pray deliverance for this tormented woman. Then I asked each passenger, "Do you know how to pray for someone who is acting like this to be delivered?"

No one answered, "Yes," but a couple of them said, "I've seen it done before and I would be glad to join with you."

In the near-empty bus about four or five of us began praying over the troubled soul. By now she was cursing, screaming, and hollering. We called on the blood of Jesus to protect everyone who was on this trip and for the power of the Holy Spirit to free this women from every attack of the enemy.

We were praising the Lord and worshiping Him with our hands lifted heavenward. Yet, she continued acting like a demon.

A DEEP, DEEP SLEEP

In truth, we didn't know the words to say, but we asked God to set her free.

We prayed for quite a while,
but nothing changed—she remained
the same uncontrollable woman.

Then I asked God Almighty, in the name of Jesus, to seal her with peace and quietness until we got to Pittsburgh. Surely those who worked with Ms. Kuhlman would know what we should do.

As I was praying, the woman fell asleep and never opened her eyes until we reached our destination—not even at the rest areas and when we stopped at restaurants.

It was early in the morning when we arrived in Pittsburgh. We had to physically help the woman walk to the place where we stood in line waiting for the doors of the church to open at 9:00 A.M. to get into the service. She was even sleeping standing up—and we took turns holding onto her. She didn't utter a word or make a move.

Once inside, I appointed a couple of people to stay with her, and in my heart I knew everything was going to be all right.

Between the time of waiting and the lengthy service, we were there practically the entire day. While I was helping with the service, I kept my eyes on those who were on our bus—and not one of them was healed.

Ms. Kuhlman gave the benediction, the service was over, and we were back on the bus. To be honest, many were greatly discouraged that they had not received their miracle.

NO HELP FROM FRANK

I could hardly believe it, but the lady who had caused such a commotion was still fast asleep. It was perplexing—nothing like any of the charter bus trips I'd ever led before.

One of the first things we do after such a long journey is to look for a restaurant large enough to serve a bus full of people. When we stopped, I found a pay phone and called my husband—which I rarely did on these trips.

I said, "Frank, have everyone pray" (we had a lot of prayer warriors in St. Louis who called on God for those making these journeys). Then I told him, "We have a woman traveling with us who I believe is filled with demons. We've asked God to seal her off and not let her utter a word or do anything disruptive like her behavior was on the way to Pittsburgh." I added, "She's been in a deep sleep and we can't wake her up."

Even at this rest stop, the woman was still sleeping on the bus, and we had people keeping their eye on her.

"Frank," I said, "this has been an unusual trip. No one was healed, the people are grumbling, and I don't know what in the world..."

He stopped me in mid-sentence. "Joan," he countered, "don't tell me your troubles. I've got both the kids, and they each have runny noses and don't feel good. And I can't find a clean shirt for work tomorrow."

It was one of the few times I let the kids stay home with him.

Frank continued, "I don't want to hear your problems, I've got plenty of my own."

Wow! I didn't know how to respond. I thought it was important enough for him to listen, but evidently not. So I said, "Frank, that's okay. Goodbye." And I hung up the phone.

I NEEDED PERFUME!

On these excursions I was always the last one to eat and the last one to get on the bus because I had to watch over 50 or 60 individuals.

Since I was helping in the services, I physically touched hundreds of people so I needed to find a restroom to wash my hands.

When I walked in, one of the women on our bus came over

to me, saying, "Joan, I'm so sick. I feel so bad."

Quickly, I responded, "Oh, honey, splash some cold water on your face, you're probably just overtired."

Immediately, she proceeded to throw up—and it went everywhere, but mostly over me!

My secretary, Susan, was on that trip and I asked her to fetch some clean clothes from my suitcase. I stood in the washroom and almost had to take a bath—changing my shoes and all my clothes.

I refreshed myself with some perfume and hopped on the bus, waiting for everyone to come back on board. I didn't even have time to eat.

As was always the case, before every leg of the journey we prayed before proceeding on our way.

THE NUN AND THE BLIND MAN

There was a Catholic nun on this journey named Sister Mary Luke from a convent in St. Louis. She make frequent trips with us. We called her "the hitch hiking nun" because she would always ask us to pick her up at different locations. It made us wonder if she had permission to leave her convent, but we loved her just the same.

Sister Mary Luke always brought a small stringed instrument like a lap harp. She also had a folding music stand which she would place in the aisle. Seated next to her on this trip was a blind man named Mr. Simons. She took his hand and showed him how to turn the pages of her music book whenever she told him.

I smile every time I visualize the scene.
But our mission was dead serious. These
people needed miracles from God.

Also on the bus was a deaf woman who worked at the Concordia Lutheran Seminary library.

WERE THESE PEOPLE NUTS?

Once everyone was on board, I picked up the microphone and prayed that the Lord would touch each individual—that the deaf would hear, the blind would see, and the lame would walk.

We had a long, long journey ahead and we were still believing God for the miracles we came for.

After our time of prayer, I started walking down the aisle and Mr. Simons, the man who was blind, suddenly commented, "Oh, oh. There's a fragrance in this bus."

Sister Mary Luke immediately spoke up, "It's the fragrance of the Holy Spirit. I am experiencing it too."

They had their hands raised, praising the Lord.

When I reached the next seat, the deaf woman from the seminary library, exclaimed, "I smell that fragrance. I've never smelled anything like that before!"

As you may have heard, when a person who is deaf or hard of hearing begins to talk, it is usually in a very loud voice because they don't think you can hear what they're saying.

I knew she could read lips, so I said, "No, honey, that's not the Holy Spirit. I just put fresh perfume on back at the restaurant."

She said, "No, no. It's something else."

Next, I passed by a man who had a crippled leg. He asked, "What is that fragrance?"

As I continued to walk, I kept hearing the same words, but I repeated, "No, it's me!"

This trip had been strange, but now I thought these people were all going nuts!

HEALED AND DELIVERED

When I reached the woman who had been in a dead sleep for so very long, all of a sudden she woke up. Then she raised her hands and started praising God.

I couldn't believe my eyes. The news traveled through the bus like lightning. Within seconds, they all began praising, and worshiping the Lord.

I thought the whole bus was going to lift off the highway!

Then up toward the front I heard someone yelling. It was the woman from the Concordia library shouting, "I can hear. I can hear everything perfectly!"

Mr. Simons was next! "Oh, I can see. I can see the highway—and the trees!"

Sister Mary Luke, was still strumming her lap harp, and there was a radiant glow on her face.

The Holy Spirit permeated every seat in that bus. Each person who had a sickness or infirmity was healed.

Even the woman who was exhibiting demonic activity was

completely delivered. Hallelujah!

Leonard, who arranged for her to be with us, later met her at many real estate meetings and was thrilled to report that her life had completed turned around.

GOD'S SPIRIT IS WITHIN YOU

Here is what every believer needs to know. We all have the power of the Holy Spirit and it is up to us to pray through any circumstance or situation. We don't need to depend on anyone else.

Regarding the lady who we believe was possessed by demons, I was personally convinced that she would be delivered during the service in Pittsburgh. However, her healing didn't happen there.

God let me know, "Joan, you have the greatest power living inside of you that has ever been known. It is My Holy Spirit. Exhort the authority that you have!"

As long as I live, I will never forget this journey. As the fragrance of God's Spirit touched these people, they were all healed and delivered. It certainly wasn't my perfume!

The Lord showed me that we don't have to "chase" the Spirit of God by running here and there. Yes, it is wonderful to be in a place where His presence is powerful and people are in one accord, but we need to understand that the Kingdom of God dwells inside each of us as believers.

At this very moment, even if you are alone, you can call on Him for the miracle you need.

Four

DADDY'S BIRTHDAY PRESENT

My son, give attention to my words;
Incline your ear to my sayings. Do not let
them depart from your eyes; keep them in the
midst of your heart; for they are life to those
who find them, and health to all their flesh.

– PROVERBS 4:20-22

*A*fter Kathryn Kuhlman asked me to be part of her ministry, she gave me the great privilege of arranging the details of her meetings in St. Louis. I did this for many years, from 1966 until the end of 1976.

During this period I was taking chartered buses every week to Pittsburgh, Pennsylvania, with sick and infirmed people who wanted to attend her healing services. The miracles we saw are far too numerous to count. We witnessed changed lives and it was absolutely tremendous what God allowed us to see.

At the time, our two children, Kimmy and Michael, were small. So, not wanting to leave them, I hired a tutor to accompany us on the bus. Frank stayed home because of his work, but our children loved the trips. They would sit in the back with the tutor, an energetic young lady who taught them so much.

SUCH A LONG JOURNEY

One morning I received a phone call from a woman who shared with me that her child, Leslie, had cancer in her leg.

She told me, "I would love to go to Pittsburgh with you, but Leslie is in the hospital and won't be released for a couple of days. I will have to wait and see if she will be able to handle such a long journey."

———————————⋅⨟⋅———————————

The bus trip to Pittsburgh was 600 miles. With the rest stops we made, it took nearly 18 hours one way.

A few days later I had a call from the mother that Leslie was now home, but that the radiation treatments she had received caused her leg to become severely burned and very swollen—much larger than her other leg. She was a very frail, sick young girl.

Yet, the parents, full of faith, were determined for their daughter to go with us to one of Ms. Kuhlman's healing services in Pittsburgh.

A BIRTHDAY WISH

We reserved seats on the bus for the mother and daughter, who lived quite a distance from St. Louis. The father was going to drive them to our departure point, at a shopping center from where we always left in the middle of the night.

The bus filled up while we were waiting for them. When their car arrived, the father opened the side door and lovingly lifted his precious daughter with his strong arms.

Little Leslie, who weighed about 60 or 70 pounds, was wearing a coat and had gloves on her hands. He gently brought her into the bus. We had reserved a seat near the front for her and her mom. I wanted to be close by in case there was anything the mother wanted me to help her with.

Fortunately, we had one empty seat on the bus, so I said to her mom, "Why don't you let her have the entire two seats and we will put you right in front of her."

Her father laid her down so gently and the mother pushed a pillow underneath the leg that was so swollen. The flesh, because of the radiation, looked horrible.

As they made her comfortable and tucked her in, we heard this child say to her father, "Daddy, I know your birthday is Friday and I won't be home. I'll be in the Miracle Service." Then she added, "I haven't bought you a gift, but I'm going to bring a present home from Pittsburgh for you."

He responded, "Oh, that will be fine."

Then Leslie added, "Daddy, I'm going to be healed. Jesus is going to heal me and that will be my present to you."

I can tell you there wasn't a dry eye on the entire bus.

The father bent over, kissed his daughter, and told her how much he loved her—and that while she was gone he would be praying for her healing.

THE EFFECTS OF RADIATION

Just before the bus pulled out, we asked the Lord for safety on the road and that His healing work would be accomplished.

On the journey, some drifted off to sleep, others were praying quietly, and a few were singing praise and worship songs to the Lord.

There was little Leslie, propped up to make her as comfortable as possible. I could see that one leg was full of fluid and was severely swollen. From the knee down it looked as though you had taken a piece of dark leather and wrapped it around her leg.

Her other limb was so tiny you could put your hand around it and touch your thumb and forefinger.

She had cute shoes on and a sock on the cancer-ridden leg. A little while into the trip we heard Leslie start to cry. She complained that her leg was hurting, so her mom and I went to her seat. Her mother said, "Honey, I think the sock is too tight for your leg, I'm going to take it off."

She slowly removed her shoe and then proceeded to take off the sock as gently as she could. As she did, it pulled off some of the flesh.

A piece of black, burned flesh fell into her daughter's sock. There was a gaping hole that went down the shin bone and you could see right inside her leg. I am sorry to be so graphic, but this is what I saw.

The mother had some gauze and she wrapped the wound carefully before putting the little slipper back on.

Her mom was so loving and caring. She tried to entice her daughter to eat some snacks, including pieces of an orange and potato chips, but Leslie had no appetite.

DISABLED DAVID

As we continued toward Pittsburgh, all I could think of was

this precious child.

———————— ✍ ————————

I could only imagine what someone so
young and innocent must be thinking.

Seated right across the aisle was a man named David, who was obviously in pain, but he would try to say encouraging things to Leslie. This severely disabled man had two small boys of his own at home.

David had been a heavy equipment operator for the highway department. His job was to cut grass and do landscaping treatment on the sides of the roadways. It usually involved working on a tremendous slope. One day a large piece of equipment rolled over, pinned him underneath the machinery, and pushed him down into the ground.

His back was severely injured. He couldn't even lift up a cup of coffee without experiencing excruciating pain—and the doctors told him they had done everything they could.

David could no longer play with his children and could hardly stand because the discomfort was too intense. This agony went on for several years.

A TOUGH DECISION

His mother-in-law heard about the bus going to a Miracle Service in Pittsburgh, Pennsylvania. She asked him to go, but his reaction was, "No, I could never do that. I can't even go to the grocery store, much less get on a bus."

Believing God would heal him, she insisted, "David, please, I want you to go."

He kept refusing until, desperate, she told him, "If you don't, I am going to stop supporting you and your family financially."

Now he was between a rock and a hard place, because he depended on her income.

The son-in-law reluctantly agreed to make the trip, but he was moaning and groaning except for the times he would say something pleasant to Leslie.

EXCHANGING NOTES

As the leader of the bus, I always had a seat up front, but constantly walked up and down the aisle, talking to one person after another because they all had special needs.

At one point I was sitting next to the bus driver talking about the next stop we would make when I was handed a handwritten note on a scrap of paper. It read, "This is David. I am in too much pain, Please stop this bus. I want to get off."

I looked at the note and prayed, "Lord, give me wisdom. What should I do? His wife, children, and mother-in-law have kissed him goodbye. They are all believing You for a miracle."

I turned the paper over and wrote a note back to him: "David, I cannot let you off the bus. We are not in a location where you could get transportation home. So you're going to have to be strong and stay with us. I will come and pray for you in a moment."

After my conversation with the bus driver, I walked back to David and said, "We can't stop. Honey, I'm so sorry you are in pain, but let's all pray."

"No, I don't want any prayer," he answered, defiantly.

"Well, that's what we have to offer and Jesus is here," I told him. "Can't you feel His presence?"

"No! I don't feel anything except pain. I want off this bus."

"David, that isn't possible. Your family paid for your bus ticket to be here and we've been asked to get you to the service so God can heal you."

OH, HOW WE PRAYED

To put it mildly, he had an absolute fit. He was determined to get off when we stopped for food and find a way home, but he could hardly lift his own legs. So I reiterated, "David, we're going to pray for you right now."

I asked a couple of the women to join with me. Together, we laid hands on him and we fervently prayed.

When we had finished, I turned to walk back to the front, there was Leslie across the aisle—her eyes big as saucers. She was watching and listening to everything.

As the bus rolled on, every now and again, David would say something sweet to her. She was telling him that she couldn't wait to be healed—and how she would be able to play with her daddy and walk with her momma.

HOW WOULD WE GET INSIDE?

At the next rest stop, we helped David off the bus and into the restaurant. His attitude changed and he seemed actually glad to get back on the bus and into a soft seat.

After 18 hours we arrived at First Presbyterian Church in Pittsburgh where Ms. Kuhlman held her weekly service. The crowd waiting to get in was enormous.

There were people on the steps, the sidewalk, the church yard, even on the other side of the street.

I prayed, "Lord, we've traveled so far. Please let there be room for all of us."

David was still complaining about his pain and I said to the women seated near me, "Let's pray for David one more time before we disembark."

I knew we would have to walk at least half a block down the street and stand there for a long time waiting for the doors to open. This was a serious concern. I had seen people turned away before because of the crowds.

As we walked back to pray for David, all of a sudden he started screaming: "I have no pain! I have no pain! I have no pain!"

He jumped out of his seat and started running up and down the aisle of the bus. People were shouting for joy and praising the Lord. It was absolutely awesome. As you can imagine, our faith was sky high.

Little Leslie was wide-eyed. She began crying, "Mom, he is healed!" Then she turned to him and said, "Mr. David, you're healed." It was a beautiful scene.

OVER THE TOP!

When David finally gained his composure, he turned to Leslie and told her, "Now don't you worry about getting in that church. I'm going to make sure you get in."

On the street-level sidewalk of the 100-year-old sanctuary there was a big rock wall topped by an iron picket fence with sharp points.

David said, "Do you know what I'm going to do?" Leslie and her mother were listening intently. "I'm going to climb over that wall, then lift you and your mom to the other side."

What an aggressive agenda! God had miraculously healed him. There was no more pain and he no longer believed in impossibilities. He was willing to do whatever it took to get Leslie into the service.

I agreed. And so did the bus driver, who said, "David, I'll give you a hand."

So Leslie, her mother, David, and myself got out of the bus and made our way to the imposing rock wall. The driver cupped his hands, David used them as a step as he grabbed the picket fence and climbed over.

"Let's take Leslie first," he said from the other side. As we held her frail little feet in our hands, David was leaning over the fence—those sharp pickets could have stabbed him in a heartbeat. An hour earlier, this short man who weighed about 155 pounds couldn't lift a cup of coffee. Now he was exclaiming, "Lift her up! Lift her up!"

We kept raising her higher and higher, then all of a sudden she was within his reach. We took every precaution we could because of the severity of her condition.

David grasped her securely underneath her arms and carefully lifted her over the iron fence. What a sight!

Those from our bus were screaming and shouting encouragement—and so was everyone watching the scene.

---

*The onlookers had no idea what
was wrong with this little girl, but they
knew this man was bound and determined
for her to be in the service.*

Then David turned to Leslie's mom, "Come on. Let me lift you, too."

So we repeated the process and helped her over the fence. To me, the miracle was that when the doors opened, everyone on our bus was able to get inside.

Over time, I had been asked to help Ms. Kuhlman during the services in Pittsburgh as well as all the services on the road in other states. However, this didn't give me the right for those I brought to have preferential seating in Pittsburgh. But we had reserved seating in all the out-of-state crusades.

I worked with her assistants, Ruth Fisher and Maggie Hartman. It was as if the Lord gave me all the guidance I needed for such a ministry. I watched, listened, and learned how to follow God's Holy Spirit and what He spoke to me. I was quick to respond—as I am even today.

WHO WAS CRYING?

That day, after the music started, Ms. Kuhlman came out on the platform. She was very particular about never allowing a sound from the audience in her services. No children crying or people walking in and out creating a disturbance.

All of a sudden I heard the whimper of a child and thought "Where did that come from?"

Maggie, Ruth, and I were looking everywhere, on all sides of the auditorium. I quickly recognized that the sound was from the front of the church. So I very quietly walked down a side aisle, trying not to be noticed.

I looked across the pews and about four rows back I spotted Leslie, her mom, and David seated on that row. Although Ms. Kuhlman loved children, she never liked to have them seated close to the front because of their natural tendency to be noisy.

It was Leslie who was crying—a gentle cry, not loud or screaming. But I didn't know what to do.

As Ms. Kuhlman looked over at the fourth row, I was worried that she was going to ask the ushers to remove the girl. Suddenly, Leslie's mother began to cry.

But instead of stopping the service, Ms. Kuhlman came down off the platform and walked over to where Leslie, her mom, and David were seated. "What's happening here?" she wanted to know.

David spoke up, "This little girl has cancer. Her leg was split open, and now we are watching something happen that we don't understand."

"Quick, Please Look at This"

Ms. Kuhlman had a doctor from John Hopkins University who was always present at her meetings. She turned to him and said, "Come over here. Quick, please look at this."

Overwhelmed by the power of God as he looked at Leslie's leg, the physician exclaimed, "Ms. Kuhlman, I can't even imagine this happening, but if you will just look, the flesh is brand new that's being formed inside of the crevice that was in this child's wounded leg. New pink flesh is growing."

There are very few moments in life when you see something so incredible with your own eyes. Leslie was being healed right on the spot. And the physician was almost beside himself as he described what was happening.

———————— *◈* ————————

It was a moment of glorious praise.

GOD TOOK OVER

After the service was over and Leslie was back on the bus, everything about her had changed. She could walk on her leg and sit down like a normal child. In fact, she and her mom giggled all the way home.

It took longer than usual to reach St. Louis, because when we stopped in restaurants we spent so much time rejoicing and praising the Lord for what He had done.

David, whose pain had disappeared, was more excited about Leslie's healing than his own! Nearly everyone on the bus who had been sick were now healed and made whole.

Here was a girl who had been given absolutely no hope and the doctors had no answers. But now God had taken over and was replacing that burned flesh with new skin. She was destined for death, but the Lord had made her whole.

When we arrived back at the shopping center parking lot, Leslie's dad was waiting. At that time it wasn't easy to call long distance, so he knew nothing about the miracle that had taken place. But the joy of everyone on the bus was contagious. Their hearts were full and running over.

The door of the bus flew open and the dad jumped inside, running to his little girl. Immediately, she began singing, "Happy birthday to you. Happy birthday to you."

She jumped into her father's arms and exclaimed, "Daddy, I brought my present back for you!"

Just repeating this story, the goose bumps on my arms seem as big as golf balls! I can still see God mending that leg like

JOAN GIESON

putty going into the crack of a wall—and finishing it off with a beautiful coat of fresh paint.

The Greatest Gift

Three days later Leslie and her mother drove to St. Louis to our home so I could see once again what God had done. Both legs of this child were now the same size, and she could run and jump as she did before cancer invaded her body. Her leg had the healthy pink glow of a brand new baby.

Yes, Leslie's daddy got his best birthday present ever!

Our God is so awesome. He is everything.

If you are struggling today with an impossible situation:

- A crisis that seems to never end.
- A problem you think will take you to the grave.
- A condition that no one has an answer, a pill, or a bandage to cover.

Turn it over to Jesus.

There is a reason you are reading these words. My prayer is that you can feel His powerful presence as we are talking about our Father, His Son, Jesus, and His Spirit—that brings life to our very existence.

Imagine for a moment Leslie returning home and playing with her siblings and friends and going back to school. Can you picture a child who was given a death sentence now being given newness of life?

Whether it is a terminal illness, a financial difficulty, a misunderstanding, a broken heart, a lack or loss of anything, there is always hope. Perhaps a traumatic event you had absolutely nothing to do with marred your childhood. You were just an innocent victim. Well, you need not carry that stigma any longer.

The story you have just read is one I saw with my own eyes. And I know a miracle is waiting for you.

Friend, don't let the Lord and your miracle pass you by. Reach out and touch Him. Take hold of His hand and tell Him what you need. Turn your problem over to the Master and according to His Word it will be solved. This very moment He is waiting to hear from you.

Five

"THAT'S MINE!"

*Now this is the confidence that we have in Him, that
if we ask anything according to His will, He hears us. And if
we know that He hears us, whatever we ask, we know that
we have the petitions that we have asked of Him.*

– 1 JOHN 5:14-15

The first charter bus we took from St. Louis to Pittsburgh
to attend Kathryn Kuhlman's services was in 1966. It was just
after I had received a personal healing in one of her meetings
and was now on fire for God.

Actually, I only told a few people about the upcoming trip,
but within a week every seat on the entire bus was reserved
—and many who were going with us had serious physical
problems.

One gentleman on the trip was a leading educator in our St.
Louis public schools. He had a chronic heart condition.

I did not know the man, but some friends had visited him
in the intensive care unit of a local hospital and his heart had
literally given out. He was on oxygen around the clock and
they didn't expect him to live.

His friends told him, "There is a bus going to a miracle
service in Pittsburgh, Pennsylvania, and we think that you
should be on it. We'd like for you to pray about going." They
told him of healing testimonies they had heard.

"There's a woman taking a bus to this meeting," they informed him, "and if you would like for us to call her and see if there's any space available we will be happy to do that for you."

He immediately agreed. However, his wife was very adamant about him not going because she was frighted of him leaving intensive care for such a long trip. "What if there is an emergency?" she wanted to know. But he insisted on going.

When they called, there were only two seats available, and I suggested that someone travel with him. But his wife and other members of the family refused to have anything to do with the idea. He would be making the trip alone.

His brother, however, agreed to pick him up from intensive care and drive him to the departure point for the bus.

On a very cold morning, we saw the gentleman coming with his large oxygen unit and a breathing mask. He was almost the last person to board. He still had a medical tag around his wrist, and a hospital gown under the jacket and slacks he was wearing.

As I welcomed him, I could see that the man's color was a bluish gray, almost green. He looked like death itself. I sent up a silent prayer, "Dear God, let this man be healed."

We found a seat for him near the rear of the bus.

WAS HE ALIVE?

During our rest stops, he didn't have the strength to leave the bus. He just laid his head back and rested. On the journey, every once in a while, I would walk past his seat and lightly touch him to see if he would open his eyes—because it was difficult to tell if the man was dead or alive. He looked that bad.

Having been to Ms. Kuhlman's meetings, I knew we needed

to arrive in the middle of the night to make it into the church. The streets filled up with vehicles bringing the sick and afflicted. Some arrived in ambulances. Others were in the back of station wagons—so ill they had to lay down.

In the early morning hours, the passengers on our bus waited outside for the doors to open, including this brave soul with his oxygen tank and breathing mask.

The atmosphere was electric. People were singing and praising the Lord as the sun was rising.

Once inside, we helped this man find a seat about the third row from the platform. I kept my eyes on him as much as possible.

As the organ and piano music began, I couldn't help but think, "This must be what heaven will be like."

"THAT'S WHAT I HAVE COME FOR"

In this divine atmosphere, I saw the man's head slowly perk up. He was watching intently as Ms. Kuhlman walked onto the solid marble platform of the First Presbyterian Church.

She didn't welcome the audience or even say, "I'm Kathryn Kuhlman. The first words out of her mouth were: "There's someone right here who is being healed of a terminal heart disease"—and she pointed her long finger straight at the man we had brought with us.

Well, like a jack-in-the-box, this man jumped to his feet. "That's mine! That is what I have come for," he shouted. "That's mine!"

He took the oxygen mask off and we watched his color

turn from blue to pink We saw him take many deep breaths without difficulty and knew he was healed.

Ms. Kuhlman didn't bring him up to the front as she often did. She just went on to the next miracle.

His healing seemed so natural and easy for this educated man. While he was praying, he received everything he asked for. It was just like making a list for the grocery store!

On the way back to St. Louis he was grinning like a Cheshire cat! He hadn't brought a change of clothes, so he returned the way he came—with one huge difference. He returned home with the miracle that saved his life.

Many years later we learned that the gentleman had been promoted to higher positions in education and we were so happy to have been part of his journey.

The love of God that passes all understanding is yours and mine. Don't be timid. Reach out and take the miracle you need. It's there—waiting for you.

Your heavenly Father has enough for all of us; there will never be a shortage of His blessings and favor. Because you are His child, He will never forget or forsake you. As scripture tells us, if we know how to give good gifts, He knows how to give so much more (Luke 11:13).

God loves you unconditionally.

Six

AN AMAZING DAY AT ROCKAWAY BEACH

I shall not die, but live, and
declare the works of the Lord.
– PSALM 118:17

Several months after Ms. Kuhlman went home to be with Jesus, I felt led to accept invitations and speak in different cities and even overseas. The services were marvelous. I did this until I began working in Benny Hinn's crusades.

In Indiana, 27 churches united together and rented the civic auditorium. I was the speaker for two nights.

The place was packed to capacity with several thousand people present and miracles happened just as they did in Kathryn Kuhlman's meetings.

At the time, I had been traveling for a while and was thinking, "Lord, I really need a rest. I just need a few days off to recoup and regroup."

Thankfully, my family was able to join me for the Indiana meetings and after the final service I went back to the hotel with them for a bite to eat. No sooner were we in our room when the phone rang; the call was from a woman I didn't know.

She said, "Hi. My name is Diane Shelton. We have a little

cottage down at Rockaway Beach. We'd like to invite you and your husband to spend a few days there."

She described the location on the White River near Branson in southwest Missouri. "You can spend as much time as you would like there, it's wonderful. We have a small boat tied up at the dock—and there will be food in the refrigerator. I think you'll like it."

We accepted her kind invitation and they told us where to find the key.

FISHING OR SHOPPING?

Frank and I returned to St. Louis the next day and didn't waste any time. We asked our daughter Kim to join us—she was about 14 years old at the time

So we packed our suitcases and away we went to Rockaway Beach. However, when we reached our destination and pulled into the driveway, there was a car already parked there. We thought perhaps they left an extra vehicle for their getaways.

We walked to the front door, and to our surprise, were greeted by the woman who had extended the invitation. She threw her arms around us and gave us a big welcome. "My husband and I decided to drive down from Indiana to tidy up the house and make it ready for you."

We were delighted to see them since there was plenty of room in the cottage. They had prepared some food for us and the men were already talking about the good fishing a stone's throw away. Frank couldn't wait to get out on the boat—and that's what they did, taking along the Shelton's big dog.

Women much prefer shopping, so the three of us decided we would drive to a nearby town—there weren't many stores in Rockaway Beach.

When we were ready to leave, our hostess discovered she

didn't have the keys to their car—and I didn't have mine either. The men had driven off with both sets.

This didn't seem to bother Diane. She said, "There's a friend of ours who owns a motel up the street. I'm sure he will let us borrow his car." The man was a retired Assemblies of God missionary.

So Diane, Kimmy, and myself walked over and he welcomed us in. He was a rather cranky old guy who never stopped working around the motel. He and his wife cleaned the rooms, did the landscaping, and managed the front desk.

"OH, MY GOODNESS!"

Immediately, the elderly missionary began sharing stories of his journeys. I sensed that he was rather disheartened about his former missionary life—there was meager financial support and he saw few results for his effort.

I felt sorry for him since we had just finished a glorious crusade in Indiana.

Then the man started talking about the Baptist preacher who lived next door. "He doesn't believe in the baptism of the Holy Spirit and healing, and thinks he's the only one who's going to make it to heaven. So we're not talking to each other any more."

It was getting rather late, so I said, "Let's just have a word of prayer before we go."

My back was to the window, but Diane, Kimmy, and the missionary could see the street—and at about the same time, their jaws dropped and they were exclaiming, "Oh, my goodness. What's happening out there?"

I quickly turned around and saw an elderly woman stretched out in the middle of the road. I didn't know if she had been hit by a passing car, had fallen, or what had happened. "Let's go and see if we can help."

When we rushed outside, a man about 50 years old was standing next to her, looking extremely concerned. "Sir, what happened? I wanted to know.

"She's dead," he responded.

"How do you know?" I asked.

"There's no pulse. There's no breath," he said. "I've checked it all. She's not responding to anything,"

The situation looked very serious. She was motionless.

"SHE'S DEAD"

Immediately, I felt led to say, "I don't believe God would want this lady to die in the middle of the street like this."

The man shot back, "She's dead. Just leave her alone."

"Sir, I'm going to pray for her." So I quickly fell down on my knees and leaned over this sweet old lady. I wasn't a nurse, had never taken CPR, and knew nothing about reviving someone, but I put my hands on her chest just like I had seen people do on television—and made some up and down movements.

Then I prayed, "In the Name of Jesus. I bind the spirit of death and call on the Spirit of life to return to her body and give her life once again."

Nothing happened. The man protested, "Please, please leave her alone. She's dead."

Again, I repeated, "I don't feel God wants her life to end like this. I don't know what's happened here, but I believe this woman will live."

Despite the man's objections, I told Diane and Kimmy to lift and rub her legs to try and get some circulation flowing. In the meantime I was still pushing on her chest and breathing into her mouth. And I kept praying, "In the Name of Jesus, you will not die. You will live and give glory to God."

At that moment, as I was still kneeling over the woman, I felt myself leaning on someone I didn't recognize at all. Then, on the other side of me was the discouraged, retired Pentecostal missionary. All three of us were kneeling together, praying for this woman.

I turned to the gentleman I didn't recognize and asked, "Who are you?"

I was surprised to learn he was the Baptist preacher who lived next door—the one who didn't believe in healing. But there we were, praying for God to raise a dead woman back to life.

Within just a few minutes, we saw the woman's eyes flicker and open—she had the most beautiful blue eyes.

A GREAT LIGHT

In the background I heard the sirens of emergency vehicles approaching, but I started talking with her, cradling her head in my arms. "You've been with Jesus. Did He tell you anything?" I asked.

In her half-dazed condition, she softly answered, "I only saw this great light and He said He loved me. And that's enough for me."

"He told you He loved you?" I asked in amazement.

"Yes, and I feel His love everywhere," she added. "I feel filled with God's love."

"What is your name? I asked. "And where are you from?"

"Gracie," she answered. "I am from Kansas City and am here on a holiday."

About that time, an ambulance arrived and two men rushed over with a stretcher. They began to ask what was going on.

The man who had been with the woman when we first arrived on the scene, answered, "I don't know what happened, but I knew she was dead. She had no pulse. But now she is breathing."

The attendants rolled her into the ambulance and drove to the hospital.

Standing there in the street, Diane, my Kimmy, the missionary, the Baptist preacher, and I were all shouting praises to the Lord.

When I looked around there was a crowd that had gathered—and they had been watching the entire time.

We who had been praying were filled with love and joy. To see a person return from death to life is overwhelming, but in reality it should be an everyday occurrence.

I turned to the Baptist preacher, "What do you think about this?"

"I never believed it could happen, but I saw it with my own eyes. The woman was dead and I watched as life surged back into her."

The missionary was like a 16-year-old boy. He was jumping up and down and praising God. Even some of the onlookers were clapping their hands and shouting for joy.

THE SEQUENCE OF EVENTS

Diane, Kimmy, and I forgot about shopping. We headed back to the cottage and waited for the men to arrive.

It was quite a while before they (and the dog) returned.

We were anxious to tell our story, but before we could open our mouths, my husband said, "You'll never believe what happened to us."

They told us how they went quite a way down the river. Evidently Mr. Shelton knew a special spot where fish would jump into the boat without catching them—a likely fish story!

Well, on this day, they ran out of gas. It was fall and most of the resorts in the area had closed down for the season and there was hardly anyone around. Frank explained, "We hollered and shouted, but no one heard us. We were drifting for a long time, but eventually we floated to shore and walked up to a small cottage, but it was empty."

Fortunately, they spotted a can of gas, filled the engine on the boat, then left some money in the handle of the gas can with a note: "Thank you. We've used your gas"—and Mr. Shelton gave his name and phone number.

Then they returned to Rockaway Beach, docked the boat and walked to the cottage.

As they related the story, I could see the hand of God and how He had the whole thing planned.

The Lord knew from the beginning that the woman was going to die in the middle of the street. He also knew the men were going fishing, so He had to prevent them from returning, because if they had, and given us the keys to the car, we would have gone shopping and never walked to the missionary's motel—where the chain of events took place.

WE HAD TO LAUGH

After listening to their story, we told the men, "Well, if you think you had an adventure, listen to what we did." They were absolutely amazed at the miracle.

A few hours went by as we talked about how God had everything under control. Then the five of us decided to jump in the car and find a place to eat.

On the way, we made a stop at a small general store across from the missionary's motel. The minute we walked in, the storekeeper started talking. "You should have been here this afternoon to see what happened."

Excitedly, she told us, "One of the locals, who is a registered nurse, breathed life into a dead woman who was laying right in the middle of the street."

We had to laugh. I am not a registered nurse, and I am not from Rockaway Beach! But this is how stories get embellished.

After our meal, we decided to drop by the hospital and find Gracie, the woman whose life had been spared by God. The staff led us to her room. She had just eaten and seemed to be relaxed. "The only thing wrong with me is some soreness in my chest," she admitted, "I must have fallen the wrong way."

I chuckled inside, knowing it was me doing all that pounding!

About that time, the same 50-year-old-man who was on the street with the lady walked in. "Oh," she exclaimed, "have you met my son, Georgie?"

"Not formally," I answered, somewhat surprised.

"He's a medical doctor in Kansas City. And he brought me

on this holiday." Then she added, "When this happened, they said I died, but Georgie brought me back to life."

We all had to bite our lips to keep from saying anything. Her son had nothing to do with her recovery. All he knew was that she had passed away.

YOUR STEPS ARE PLANNED

I have thought about the scene on that street so often. Here was a man with a medical degree who saw what happened, but couldn't bring himself to admit the miracle. But God knew.

Later, I learned that the missionary and the Baptist preacher became close friends and often reflected on that amazing day.

My friend, God is on the throne and has every second of our day planned.

As you read these words you may be sitting in your favorite armchair, flying on a plane, or enjoying a vacation. Don't worry about your agenda. The Lord has your steps ordered —and if you will allow Him, He will walk you through doors you didn't expect to open. He will lead you into places you never believed you could enter.

Since you serve an unlimited God, expect the unexpected.

Seven

A BEAM OF LIGHT

Arise, shine; for your light has come!
And the glory of the Lord is risen upon you.

– ISAIAH 60:1

*D*uring the Christmas Dinners we held at Normandy Junior High School, they would always set up a desk and hook up a phone for me in the middle of the cafeteria.

Early one dark, snowy, icy morning the phone rang—one of countless calls I would receive that day.

"Is this the Christmas Party?" a man's voice asked anxiously.

"It certainly is," I enthusiastically replied.

What I heard next stunned me. "My wife wants to kill herself. We have no money and we're living in an abandoned building near Vandeventer and Jefferson. Ma'am if you could help us, we need to get something to eat."

"Stay right there," I urged him. "Stand on the corner and I'll send a car to pick you up."

Within 45 minutes the car returned with two homeless people, a man and a woman. His name was Frank and hers was Dorothy. They walked to the door and just stood there, hesitant to walk inside—even though the door was open and it was freezing outside, about 17 above zero.

It was as if their steps were frozen in time and they couldn't move. Their clothes were so filthy—it looked like they had

69

rolled around in a coal bin. The woman wore beat-up tennis shoes that did little to keep out the cold. They were frozen to the bone.

The moment I saw these two, I gently walked them in and gave them a big hug. They started crying uncontrollably. "It's going to be okay," I assured the husband and wife.

"You're in God's hands now, and your life is going to change. Don't worry," I told them.

As soon as they passed over the threshold of the door we handed them clean clothes, warm coats, and mittens. The school had shower facilities in the gym, so we took them there—and when they returned to the cafeteria they looked like totally different people. However, their eyes still told a tale of sadness.

A DOWNWARD SPIRAL

When I learned their story my heart went out to them even more. The couple were from Carbondale, Illinois, across the river from St. Louis. Frank was a successful accountant, but became hooked on drugs, which led to a tragic downward spiral. He lost his job, their home was foreclosed on, and their children were taken away by Social Services and placed into foster homes.

Now at the end of their rope they drove their car, the last possession they owned, across the bridge to St. Louis. When they ran out of gas they began living in the vehicle.

The police spotted them and issued a warning that if they didn't move, they'd be picked up for vagrancy. Desperate, they began to sell off the tires, battery, and other parts of the vehicle just to have a little cash to exist. And the husband was still using drugs.

Frank and Dorothy found an abandoned building for shelter, but hadn't eaten in five days. They wrapped themselves in discarded cardboard and newspapers so they wouldn't freeze to death.

On the fifth night, they both decided that the next day would be their last. They would take their lives. Frank awoke before dawn and walked around the block to find some more newspapers to cover his cold, hungry, despondent wife.

He was lying there with his arms around Dorothy when the sun came up. There was a crack in the wall and a small beam of light fell on the newspaper covering her. The light shone directly on a small notice in the paper.

"The Gieson Family Christmas Party for the homeless and needy will be held (date) at the Normandy Junior High School. If you would like to donate anything, call (number) and ask for Joan."

"Dorothy, wake up," Frank said, shaking his wife. "We're going to find help."

So they walked around the streets looking for any change they could find to put in a pay phone. It took them three hours, to find a quarter, which they used to dial our number. They kept calling and calling but couldn't get through because the phone hardly stops ringing in the days leading up to the Christmas Dinner.

Starving, Dorothy told her husband, "Forget the number. Just use the quarter to buy me a cookie or something to eat."

Frank promised, "I'll make one more call, and if we can't get through I'll buy a cookie." Then they planned on dying together.

That's when the phone rang and I said, "I'll send a car to get you."

What Would Jesus Do?

Frank and Dorothy were overwhelmed with the love and care shown to them by our ministry. We fed, clothed, and bathed them—but more important we hugged them, loved on them, and prayed for them. We did everything that Jesus would have done.

Next, we put this couple in a motel for three weeks, which I paid for personally because I wanted to see how serious they were about life. Every day I met with Frank and Dorothy and we read the Bible and I taught them about living the Christian life. Not only did they give their hearts to the Lord, but Frank made a commitment to get off drugs.

The beam of light that began shining through a crack in the wall of that abandoned building led them to Christ— *"the light of the world"* (John 9:5).

We gave them food and a little money, and when we were convinced they truly wanted to change the life they were living, we found both of them jobs.

Actually, they began working two 8-hour jobs daily—at a container manufacturing company during the day, and a bakery at night. We provided the transportation.

As time passed, they grew more and more excited about what Jesus was doing in their lives. They were able to rent a home, and eventually their children were brought back to them from Social Services—the family was reunited at last.

As I write this, Frank has a wonderful position with a cleaning company in St. Louis. He has never turned back to drugs, and we still rejoice at the transformation God made in this wonderful family.

Frank and Dorothy are just two reasons I still believe in miracles.

Eight

THIS TAKES THE CAKE!

*Now may He who supplies seed to the sower, and
bread for food, supply and multiply the seed you have
sown and increase the fruits of your righteousness.*

– 2 CORINTHIANS 9:10

The year 2009 marked the 50th annual Gieson Family
Christmas Celebration. They have all been remarkable in one
way or another, but I will never forget what took place in 1993.

We had rounded up volunteers to serve food and distribute
gifts for a crowd we expected to be approximately 2,000 people
who would be streaming through the Normandy Junior High
School cafeteria.

The food was ready, and for dessert there was cake which
the Theodoro Bakery had just delivered.

Early that morning, about 5:00 A.M., I asked everyone
present to join hands and pray together. There is always too
much at stake not to pray before you start any day. At these
events I check my list many times over to make sure we have
everything we need, and if not, I go to my heavenly Father in
prayer.

After we prayed I had a meeting with the principal of the
school and gave him the rundown of what was about to
happen. I told him, "We have enough to feed 2,000 people,

plenty of toys to give to all the kids, and baskets for each family to take home."

He was delighted and ran up to the registration desk to see if everyone was ready to go. They gave him a thumbs up, so he called me on the walkie talkie and said, "When you're ready to open the doors let me know."

I had just finished spreading the icing on the 20 large cakes the baker had brought and we put them into a room off the dining area for someone to cut. I completely forgot them when a young *St. Louis Post-Dispatch* newspaper reporter came in and asked if she could do some looking around and get a story for the paper.

"Everyone else is home for Christmas and I'm the only reporter available, so I just want to write a few details about your party." she told me. There was a photographer with her.

"Honey, take your liberty and do whatever you please."
She said she would not be able to stay long.

"AND IF WE RUN OUT OF ANYTHING..."

At the same time a young couple with several small children in tow asked me if there was something they could do, and my thoughts turned to the cakes. "Oh, yes," I answered, and took them to the cake room—with the reporter following us. I asked them to cut each cake into 100 pieces, put them on trays, and bring them into the dining room to be served as needed. The reporter was listening to every word.

Within moments I announced to all the volunteers in the building we were ready to open the door and start letting our guests in. I prayed and asked God to bless the fruits of our hands, and make this the most delicious food our guests had ever eaten. Then I added, "And Lord, if we run out of anything, please multiply what we have."

All of a sudden the place was overflowing with people, Christmas music was being sung, the meal was being served and the principal wore a smile on his face from ear to ear. It had been hard work for him, but he loved what we were doing. We had been working with him and his school district for many years.

A CONCERNED PRINCIPAL

Hours went by and I was so grateful everything was going well, when all of a sudden, the principal came bounding down the steps into the cafeteria and ran over to me. Almost beside himself, he exclaimed, "Joan, you told me we had only enough for 2,000 people, and from the registration desk we have already fed that many. But now there are at least 2,000 more standing outside. The police directing traffic say the cars are backed up for a mile. I'm afraid if you don't have enough for everyone there will be a riot."

I looked at him in amazement, and quickly responded, "Well, lock the doors. Don't let anyone in for a few moments. I've got to get a hotline to Jesus!"

I had to chuckle to myself because the principal was so nervous, but my mind quickly reverted back to the prayer just a few hours earlier: "And Lord, if we run out of anything, please multiply what we have." I had seen God do it once before and was sure He would do it again.

I turned on the loud speaker and asked all the volunteers in the building to come to the cafeteria immediately. They responded pronto. I shared with them, "We have no toys and no food for the extra number of guests who are now arriving. I need people who believe that God is going to multiply what we have. We must believe for this miracle."

The concerned principal was in the background, mumbling, "If we don't let them in, they'll tear this school down."

There were some doubters. I reassured them, "That's okay. Thanks for your honesty." I let them serve drinks or clean off tables. But those who were really praying with me in faith, I sent to the kitchen to dish out the food.

I turned to the principal, "Go ahead and open the doors." He was still shaking, but he did as I asked—and the people poured in.

I began exercising my faith as never before. The pans in the kitchen were empty, but I told the helpers, "There's lots of turkey and fried chicken in there."

One of the volunteers said, "We can't see it!"

By faith I replied, "Every time you put a fork in those pans there will be turkey or chicken. Start thanking Him in advance!"

By the time the day was over, every person who came had been fed. Then the volunteers gathered to have their own Christmas dinner—the leftovers. They were exhausted from such a long event.

"You've just witnessed a miracle," I told them.

"How do you know? One woman asked.

"Well, we only had enough food to feed 2,000 people. But today we fed 5,000. Plus, extra toys showed up and no child was left disappointed."

"You're Not Going to Believe This"

About this time, the husband of the young couple who had

never worked with us before came out of the cake room." (It was actually the teacher's lounge.) Tears were streaming down his face.

----------------- ✥ -----------------

"What's wrong?" I asked. I remembered he and his wife volunteering early that morning. I hoped no one had been stabbed with a cake knife!

"Mrs. Gieson," he continued, "You're not going to believe this."

"Believe what?" I wanted to know.

He asked me to walk with him to the cake room, saying, "It's a miracle!"

Then I looked over and saw the reporter from the *Post-Dispatch*—the one who was supposed to stay for only five minutes. I was so busy I hadn't noticed her, but she was still there, eight hours later. "How do you ever find people to work like this?" she asked me. "I've never seen anything like this in my life."

She was there when we prayed and asked God to multiply the food if necessary.

"OPEN THE BOXES!"

Earlier that day, there were twenty large sheet cakes in boxes, stacked one on top of the other. We had iced them before the young husband and his wife with two kids showed up to volunteer. We put them in that room because it was an easy job. All they were asked to do was to cut them, put the squares of cake on plates, place them on trays, and bring them out to the dining area.

Now this couple were crying tears of joy. "Mrs. Gieson, "

the man said, "open the boxes."

When we did, the same 20 cakes we had in the morning were still there—absolutely untouched! Each had been cut into 100 pieces, enough for 2,000 people. Yet there was still cake at every table.

The news photographer from the *Post-Dispatch* had taken pictures of the guests eating the cake. There had been 2,000 servings of chicken, turkey, dressing and all the trimmings. Yet we fed 5,000.

The news reporter wrote a full page story documenting the miracle which happened that day. Let me share this excerpt of the Christmas, 1993 *St. Louis Post-Dispatch* article:

Family's Dinner For 5,000 Needy Takes The Cake
By Lia Nower, *Post-Dispatch* staff

Christmas came early for the Gieson family and about 5,000 of their friends. Last Sunday, Joan and Frank Gieson and their two children rounded up volunteers from as far away as Arkansas and served up food and gifts for thousands of needy people who streamed through the Normandy Junior High School cafeteria.

This was the annual Gieson Family Christmas celebration, which has grown from inviting a few homeless people over for dinner to planning a feast for a crowd. There was fried chicken, turnip greens, sweet potatoes and dressing and much more cake than anyone realized. "Did I tell you the story about the cake?" asked Joan Gieson, who directed the action like a traffic cop from her post in the center of the room.

Gieson said she had only 20 sheet cakes when the group started serving food at about 10 A.M. "That would only feed at the most about 2,000 people," she said. "I knew we were going to run out of dessert." Instead, sheet cake appeared from nowhere—enough to feed more than twice the estimated number of guests. And, as the crowd was winding down, Gieson found that the original 20 sheet cakes were still sitting, untouched, in the kitchen.

That story might sound amazing to some, but it's pretty routine stuff for Joan Gieson—missionary, caterer, mother of two. This year, the Giesons needed toys to give the youngsters as they left for the day. Enter Terry Bruck, a Berkeley resident who heard about the dinner and decided to donate 350 stuffed animals. He then spent the day serving food while wearing a Santa hat. The Giesons needed religious music to play during dinner. Pastor Bobby Adams from the Reign of Praise Church in St. Clair, Mo., heard about the feast and packed his disc jockey equipment into the car. The Giesons needed cooks to stay up all night to prepare the meal. Ex-chef Mike Circello of Kansas City heard about the dinner and came to help.

The Giesons needed produce and money to buy chickens. Enter Carol and Charlie Nix, a couple from Little Rock, Ark., who donated thousands of dollars and drove all night to spend the day in the kitchen. "We had been in a religious crusade with Mrs. Gieson, but we didn't really know her," said Carol Nix. "The Lord has blessed us financially, so we wanted to give money to the less fortunate. Charlie said God told him to give the money to Mrs. Gieson." So the Nixes sent a check and drove to St. Louis. For Carol Nix, the experience was everything she'd hoped. "It's fantastic," she said. "I've had so much fun doing this."

If the Giesons have their way, the Christmas

extravaganza will long be a program in need of donations. "When we were little, mom was always bringing street people home," said Mike Gieson, 34. "This whole thing has really grown." Does he plan someday to take over for mom and dad? "I'll have to think about it," he said. "But, I'm afraid I'd feel too guilty if I said no."

Opening their papers, the entire city learned of this mighty miracle. Every time I read how Jesus fed the 5,000 with five loaves and two fish (Matthew 14:12-21), I am reminded of what happened that day. Hallelujah!

Nine

OUT OF THE COLD

*I was hungry and you gave Me food; I
was thirsty and you gave Me drink; I was
a stranger and you took Me in.*
– MATTHEW 25:35

It was easy to pick John out of the crowd. He was the first white man I'd ever seen with dreadlocks.

The church where I was ministering in Kansas City had a bus that would pick up the homeless on Sunday morning and promise them a hot breakfast if they would stay for the morning service.

John only came for the free food—no other reason.

I remember picking him out of the crowd, along with two of his friends. Somehow, my heart was especially drawn to them.

John was extremely shy and kept his head down so you really couldn't see his face. This seemed unusual to me.

During the service I asked John and his friends to come up to the altar for prayer, but they refused. So I walked to the back of the church and sat down next to them and was able to pray the sinners prayer as they accepted Christ as their Savior.

Underneath the braided hair and dirty clothes, John looked like a handsome man. But when I finally was able to have him look up at me I saw he did not have many teeth.

I talked with the three men, asked their names and said,

"You need some warmer clothes. After the service I want to take you to lunch. We'll go shopping after that. Will you go with me?"

Without hesitation they all said "Yes."

My husband and I finished the service and after saying goodbye to the pastor we headed toward these three men.

There they were waiting in the back corner of the church, being very quiet. They probably didn't believe my offer and were anxious to see what I would do.

I waved to them, quickly walked over and said, "Come on, gentlemen. Let's go." In a flash, we were all in the car and I was excited to see what God had in store for the day.

"LET'S GO SHOPPING"

As you have gathered reading this book, our family has been blessed by God with a heart of compassion for the homeless and this was no different. We bought them all a dinner and it was a treat to watch them enjoy their meal.

I could tell John had a difficult time eating, so I broached the topic. He told me that most of his teeth were knocked out by his father, and now the roots were infected and he was in constant pain. I felt so sorry for him and we prayed together.

True to my word, I offered, "Let's go shopping. You need new clothes and coats to get you through the winter."

At the store, the clerks were watching these street people very closely. We knew they were uncomfortable, but Frank and I reassured them that we were paying customers and everything would be all right. John and his buddies were used to being ushered out of stores like this.

We bought each of them pants, shirts, sweaters, socks, underwear, and coats. When I suggested, "Let's go to the shoe department to get some heavy-duty shoes," John quickly spoke up: "No Ma'am. You have spent enough on us already."

I was shocked he was so thoughtful regarding our money.

During the earlier service we told the congregation about our Christmas Dinner that was coming up soon in St. Louis and how many we would be feeding. Now, during our time together, these men brought up the subject briefly, asked about our family and where we lived in St. Louis.

John became so polite to me, insisting on helping me to the car, and opening and shutting the door.

I smiled to myself, seeing the confidence and change that had come over him in just one day.

We asked where they lived and at first they hesitated to tell us, but finally did. "We have a tent on the side of Intestate 70," John told us. "Just drop us off and we can walk there."

No, we wanted to drive them and their packages to the place they were living. When we reached the area, and pulled off the side of the road, they led us to their tent, hidden from view.

My heart just broke. "Please allow us to take you to a homeless shelter or pay for a couple of nights in a motel."

They refused. "We want to stay here and watch over our belongings."

A Knock at the Door

All the way back to St. Louis my thoughts were on these three men. How we could help them even more? How would they survive the elements? And so many more questions flooded my mind.

In the days following, as we were approaching the date of our Christmas Dinner, one night we were eating supper in our family room when we heard a soft knock at our front door. We couldn't imagine who it would be that late in the evening.

Frank went to the door and asked, "Can I help you?"

By this time I was at his side and saw three men dressed in nice suits, coats, and hats. I didn't recognize them for a moment, but when I did, I screamed and put my arms around all of them—John and his two friends. "Come right in," I exclaimed, "Get out of the cold."

We offered them something to eat. They took off their coats and sat down at our table. It was such a marvelous experience for us, but we were even more surprised when they told us, "We came to help any way we can at your Christmas Dinner."

We learned that shortly after we left Kansas City, the police came, ran them off the side of the highway, and threw away their tent and all their belongings.

They were crushed, but went back to the church where we met them and told the pastor how they wanted to come to St. Louis to help with our Christmas Dinner.

Of course, they needed money and clothes, so the minister gave them jobs doing repairs around the church and paid them for their services. They were able to buy some clothes and a bus ticket to St. Louis—and the next thing you know they were at our front door.

A MILLION DOLLAR SMILE!

They worked harder than any other volunteers and would not leave each night until every task was finished and the place was spotless. All three stayed at the home of our daughter and son-in-law. We made living quarters for them in her basement.

It turned out to be a six month stay for two of them—and we loved every minute. Each day they would begin by reading the Bible, concluding with verses from Proverbs and praying together.

One of the men was able to find a job as a truck driver and move into his own apartment. Another went back to the family and farm he had left. And John stayed with us the longest.

I believe God knew he needed our love and spiritual guidance. John had been on the streets since he was 3 years old, and now was in his 30's. Because of the condition of his teeth, he couldn't eat properly or chew his food.

I am thrilled to report that he lived with Kim and her family for almost three years—and became a chef in a fine restaurant in St. Louis.

An added blessing was that Kim was able to find a dentist who performed dental surgery on John, removing or repairing all his broken and infected teeth and giving him brand new ones. He now is the owner of a million dollar smile!

A HOPE AND A FUTURE

I am still overjoyed when I think of the second Christmas he was with us. John prepared our personal family dinner at our home. He shopped for all the ingredients, cooked them to perfection, waited on us—and even washed the dishes!

What a Christmas treat that was.

Thank God, John is no longer homeless, he has a career, a hope and a future. But more important, he has a personal relationship with God's Son, who removed the bitter scars of his life and gave him a brand new start.

We will always be thankful for the three wise men who came to our home from Kansas City that Christmas. They were bearing gifts of love, care, and concern. It was more than we could ask or think.

There have been many more homeless men and women who have enriched our lives. Jesus loves them just as much as He loves us.

Ten

OH, WHAT A NIGHT!

The preparations of the heart belong to man,
but the answer of the tongue is from the Lord. All
the ways of a man are pure in his own eyes, but the Lord
weighs the spirits. Commit your works to the Lord,
and your thoughts will be established.

– PROVERBS 16:1-3

*S*everal years ago we had a special dinner for the needy
and a food basket give-away. In addition to our annual
Christmas Party, this took place on Valentine's Day. We called
it the "I Love You Every Day Dinner." It was pretty neat.

When I spoke to one of the pastors who volunteered for our
Christmas Dinner about holding this event at his church, he
was excited and immediately responded "Yes." He told me he
knew an alderman from his community who would contact the
public schools and get the names of families in the district who
needed help.

I reminded the pastor, "The dinner is not about getting
votes. It's also not just about feeding people and giving them
a full basket to take home, but rather to introduce them to
Jesus." Of course, he agreed.

Our evening was to begin with registration, then a short
service in the church, including a brief teaching and an
invitation to accept Jesus Christ as Lord and Savior. Following

this, they would enjoy a delicious meal, then pick up their baskets of food to take home.

The day before the event, the pastor called to let me know the alderman had discussed the matter with the school superintendent who would not allow us to have a Christian service or to speak about Jesus if they were supplying the names of those who should attend. The food was the only thing we were to provide.

I told the pastor, "If we do what they ask, we will be totally missing the purpose of the dinner."

Meanwhile, preparations for the evening were in full swing and we went ahead as planned—not sure how things would work out.

When I walked into the building, not knowing anyone but the pastor, I jokingly said, "I'm just here to pick up my basket."

The pastor chuckled. Then he and several others shook my hand and welcomed me. When I met the alderman, I had no idea how I was going to broach the decision that he and the school superintendent had made.

However, as always, the Holy Spirit was in control. All I had to do was wait for the right time. As the Bible tells us, *"Open your mouth...and I will fill it"* (Psalm 81:10). The Spirit will speak through you.

QUESTIONS FOR THE ALDERMAN

The pastor was taking me on a tour of the new kitchen and fellowship hall and the alderman was following us. I asked the minister quietly, "Is this the gentleman who doesn't want us to say anything about Jesus?"

The pastor choked a bit, and replied, "It was the school's decision really."

I turned to the alderman and began to tell him how these dinners have transformed so many lives. I wanted him to know the potential impact. "Sir, the people are coming here tonight because they are in need. Something has happened in their lives and they are in trouble. They are searching for answers. They don't know how they can help themselves, and are coming for the assistance they so desperately need."

Then I felt led to ask the question, "Sir, do you know Jesus Christ as your personal Lord and Savior?"

"Yes, " he answered.

"Well, have you ever required help?" I wanted to know.

"Yes, I have."

"Then I continued, "Has Jesus always been at you side, giving you peace and leading you in the right direction? Has Jesus ever turned His back on you?"

"No," he assured me.

"Well, Sir. Can you say you have the secret to life, and life abundantly?"

His answer was an affirmative "Yes."

"Well, why are you keeping this from your constituents?" I wanted to know. "Why are you withholding the secret to life and not freely giving it to everyone who walks though this door? Do you believe God can't really help them, or do you think you need to keep the treasures of His word to yourself? It must be one or the other."

Next, I said, "Let me tell you a story I heard many years ago." And here is what I shared:

There were twelve of the wisest, richest men on earth, standing on top of the highest hill where they lived. One of them said, "Look down there at all our slaves."

Down below they saw countless people slaving away—working diligently for them.

The man spoke again: "One day these people will find our secret. Our secret to all love, to all wisdom, to all prosperity, to all peace and joy—our secret to all of life. And when this happens we will lose all we have here."

The second of the twelve men commented, "I believe you are right. This is what we will do. We will capsule all our secrets in a big rocket and thrust it into outer space, and no one will ever find it."

They thought for a moment, and a third man spoke up. "No," he said, "One day man will explore outer space and will surely find our secrets."

The fourth wise man chimed in: "I know what to do. We will put our secrets into a heavy container and cast it into the depths of the sea."

They all stopped and thought about the idea. Then, the fifth wise man said, "No. Surely one day someone will explore the ocean floor and they will uncover all our secrets."

After a long silence, the wisest of all the men uttered these words. "I know what we can do! We will gather all our secrets together, and we will put them into the man himself, and he will never find them."

Then I read the passage of scripture when the Pharisees came to Jesus, wanting to know where the Kingdom of God really was. Jesus could hardly believe they asked such a question, but He answered, *"The kingdom of God does not come with observation; nor will they say, 'See here!' or 'See there!' For indeed, the kingdom of God is within you."* (Luke 17:20-21).

What a profound truth. When we seek Christ, we find the answers to life.

"Sir, You Have a Choice"

"Sir," I asked the alderman with holy boldness, "do you really want your constituents to remain in the bondage they will come here with tonight? Are you afraid if they find the secrets to life that you know, they may not need you anymore? If you don't share this with them, you have become responsible for keeping them in slavery. I wonder what your Father in heaven will say when you see Him face to face?"

I continued, "What will your answer be when He asks, 'What did you give to all the men, women, and children I sent to you on that Valentine's Day? Why did you just feed them bread and meat for their stomachs, but failed to offer them the food of life? How was it, you freely received the Good News of the Gospel that truly set you free, but you did not feel led to share it with those I brought before you that special night.'"

Then I added, "If it's your job you are afraid of losing, the Lord has you in the palm of His hand. You are always on His mind. He loves you. Sir, you have a choice, as each of us do. Don't be afraid. We have the secret of life and eternity right here inside of us. His name is JESUS. I feel you must make a decision about what it is you will give to these folks tonight."

A God-Planned Emergency!

I could hardly believe those words were coming out of me! Sometimes we really don't know how strong we are in faith until we are put to the test.

I'll never forget the look on his face. He was speechless. Obviously, he was filled with fear about sharing the Gospel with these people.

Suddenly, a phone call came for him and he had to leave immediately.

As soon as he was gone, I knew exactly what we needed to do—and how to accomplish it. Oh, what a marvelous night it was. The pastor and I stood on the platform, inviting those present to come up and share a testimony, sing a song, or just to say "Thanks."

Each person had something special on their heart, just hoping others would listen. In the process, the message of Christ was proclaimed loud and clear.

After the dinner, the guests picked up
the baskets of food God had made possible
for them. What a night of memories!

At the end of the evening, the alderman returned from taking care of his emergency and thanked us for all we did. I had a big smile on my face!

HOW ABOUT YOU?

God always has the perfect plan if we are careful to follow His direction. He opens many doors of great opportunity, but if we hesitate for any reason, He will always allow someone else to fulfill the task.

We have two choices: (1) either we are in the way or (2) we can make a way. Personally, I want to be a "way maker."

How about you?

Eleven

A Honeymoon on Hold

*Bless the Lord, O my soul, and forget
not all His benefits: Who forgives all your
iniquities, Who heals all your diseases, Who
redeems your life from destruction, Who crowns
you with lovingkindness and tender mercies, Who
satisfies your mouth with good things, so that
your youth is renewed like the eagle's.*

– PSALM 103:2-5

*M*y husband, Frank, and I were married in October 1958. And in November 1959 we welcomed our first child, a son named Michael.

Then, in 1961 we had another child, Jeffery, who weighed 10 pounds. Sadly, he died at birth.

Our third child was a precious baby girl, Kim, born with black hair, hazel eyes, and long, long eyelashes. She stole our hearts the minute we looked at her.

Her brother, Mike, adored his sister and would come into the house with his little friends and peek into her crib. I watched as he showed them her tiny fingers and toes, but when they would leave, I washed her all over to make sure there were no germs lurking from their grubby hands.

Mike loved her so much and they became the best of friends as they grew up. I'm not telling you they didn't engage in sibling spats, because they did. When I would hear my son laughing a certain way I ran to see where Kim was—because I figured he had smeared her with mud or she was stuck up in a tree. Some mischief was usually going on that needed my immediate attention.

Later, as young adults, Mike owned his own business and Kim was his secretary/vice president. She worked so hard for her brother, trying to help every way she could. He not only relied on her for his business but personally as well. She would make sure his clothes were cleaned, the fridge was full and his house tidy—as well as seeing that the payroll and accounts payable were up to date.

"HI! I'M TOM"

One day, after praying each morning for a blue-eyed farmer to come and sweep her off her feet, she met him. At the time he had a job with a handyman I hired to fix our bathroom commode. I had left the key to the back door under the mat so the repairman could enter and fix the problem.

A short while later, Kim and I arrived home and as we passed the bathroom there was a blue-eyed young man wedged between the toilet and the tub. He looked up at us, smiled real big, and introduced himself. "Hi. I'm Tom. 'Pistol,' the handyman, asked me to stop by and fix your bathroom."

He had the biggest dimples I have ever seen—and it was instant love for both of them. It became a whirl-wind courtship and romance. Every day it was like sunshine radiating from her room as she got dressed and ready for work.

_____

*It was a joy just being around
her; she was so happy.*

Kimmy was swept off her feet—and still is today— with her blue-eyed farmer. The sparkle in his eyes every time he looks at her is pure love.

THE VOWS

A wedding was planned and on the big day her dad walked her down the aisle and she seemed to just float. We all stood in honor of this 22-year old virgin bride as her daddy held onto her tightly. It was difficult for him to let go of his little girl.

He kept his eyes fixed on Tommy and when he reached the end of the aisle, he stopped where the groom was standing and softly told him, "Tommy, I give you my precious daughter in marriage. Don't ever mistreat her in any way. Love, honor, and be at her side always as we have." Then he added, "But son, if you don't, I will get you!"

We laugh now, but he was dead serious. If there was ever a time for Tom to faint, that was it. But he didn't. He stood tall and immediately took responsibility.

Frank slipped Kim's hand into Tom's and blessed them as the ceremony began.

"Who gives this woman in marriage?" the preacher asked. Frank replied, "I do." He helped pull her veil back, kissed her, then turned and walked back to me.

Tears were welling in my eyes but there was a smile on my face, The man our daughter had prayed for and saved herself for was now repeating his vows, promising to love and take care of her all the days of their lives. Kim vowed to be a good and faithful wife, always at his side, and to love him forever—never finding fault but always favor.

At the end of the ceremony, the loud, thrilling sounds of the organ rang through the sanctuary. Everyone stood to their feet as the minister announced, "Now I want you to meet Mr. and Mrs. Tommy Lilley."

---

*We realized we hadn't lost a daughter,
but gained another son.*

The day was filled with pictures, lipstick kisses, flowers, formal wear, and limousines. My dad was one of the best men—looking handsome in his tux and very proud of his first grandchild to be married.

That evening at the reception, the love we felt from everyone was overwhelming. Everything was romantic and beautiful and the kids danced into the night—as did Frank and myself.

"MOM, I NEED TO TALK WITH YOU"

The honeymoon had been planned for months, but the newlyweds didn't want to leave the party. They stayed until there were only a handful of guests remaining.

Tom and Kim had reservations in one of the large downtown hotels—in the honeymoon suite. The plan was to have all the out of town guests come to our home the next morning for brunch, with the newlyweds joining us to open their gifts before heading for the airport to fly off for their honeymoon.

The next day, when Tom and Kim arrived, Kim looked as if she wasn't feeling well. But we were so glad to see the two of them that the thought of something being wrong was quickly dismissed from our minds.

It was June 4, 1989.

After brunch and opening the gifts, Kim privately pulled me aside and whispered, "Mom, I need to talk with you."

We took a few steps and she told me. "Mom, I'm having trouble walking."

My first response was. "I guess so. You danced in those high heels all night!"

"No, mom, "she responded in a serious tone, "it's not that."

I saw the expression on her face and didn't like it one bit. The next day, we called a friend who had been a guest at the wedding—a chiropractor.

"Bring her right over," he said. We did, but after looking her over he told us there was nothing he could do, but recommended that we see Dr. Dooley, a neurologist friend of his. He called and made an appointment for the next day.

WHAT COULD IT BE?

Suddenly, the honeymoon plans had to be put on hold. Kim and Tom spent the night with us and the following day we went to see Dr. Dooley.

After an examination, he said he thought it was one of three things: (1) Guillain-Barré, which could be treated with medicine, (2) Lupus, or (3) Multiple Sclerosis. Each sounded daunting.

The doctor told us, "I hope it is Guillain-Barré, but I'm pretty sure it is MS." He wanted us to make a hospital appointment through him where they would do a spinal tap and an MRI.

However, since her regular doctor was at another hospital, we wanted to call him for a second opinion and see what he advised.

As soon as possible I got alone and tried to comprehend what was taking place. Could this be real? The doctor had to be wrong. How could this be happening when just days before things were so perfect? It seemed like we were having a bad dream.

Crying, I begged God, "Father, help us, please. Her married life has just begun."

As we drove home, Kim and Tom were in shock and said very little, while Frank just quietly drove the car.

Kim's doctor made an appointment with a recommended neurologist and again the next day we were in the hospital waiting room. They had already injected some dye in her veins and we were anxious to know what would happen next.

"Mrs. Kim Lilley," a nurse called out. "Kim Lilley," she said again. We were not accustomed to hearing her married name. When Kim stood up, Tom asked if she wanted him to go with her. Of course, she did!

As the two walked out with the nurse, Frank and I just looked at one another. Our hearts were heavy— very heavy.

For the next two hours, not knowing
what was happening, we just prayed, cried,
and held onto one another.

A FRIGHTENING PROGNOSIS

Finally the door opened and we could tell by the look on the face of the nurse that something was terribly wrong. Then she said, "If you would like to talk with the doctor you can go right in. He is waiting for you."

In his office, the physician told us it was Multiple Sclerosis and that the brain and the spinal cord had lesions on them from the attack. He explained that it was a debilitating, crippling disease with no real cure. We learned that it was progressive and she had the fast moving kind. He continued, "She will probably be confined to a wheelchair."

I thought my heart was going to stop. I assured myself, "God will turn this around, I have seen Him do the impossible before—and He will fix this too."

In the weeks that followed my emotions vacillated wildly. I was strong at times, then became weaker than I could have ever imagined. I would sit by her bedside while Tommy was at work and we would talk for hours.

WAS THERE INSURANCE?

It was only a few weeks earlier that Kim and our son, Michael, called their insurance broker to see if the hospitalization policy they had at their business needed to be changed now that she was getting married.

The broker said he could offer her something that would be much better than the coverage they had for years (which included pre-existing conditions). After deciding to take his advice, they sent a cancellation for the current policy and applied for the new one with another company.

The MS was diagnosed three weeks into the new coverage. The former insurance company said they had a letter of cancellation and the new policy claimed the MS was obviously a pre-existing condition and they would not pay any of her hospital bills.

Kim was heading for expensive treatment with no insurance to cover the cost.

By Thanksgiving Day our daughter's eyesight was deteriorating and she had to use an electric wheel chair just to get around. She had severe head pain, saw double and triple, and bled from the nose every day. We watched over her 24/7, not knowing if she would make it or not.

One year went by. Every few months the home health nurse would come to the house and hook her up to an IV bottle of *Solu-Medrol*—a steroid so strong it could either, stop the attack, do nothing, or take her life. What a choice! But from time to time Kim would be so sick she would agree to take the medicine.

The nurse would bring the IV drip bottles and insert the tube in her arm and begin the five day treatment until it was over. In my wildest dreams I could never imagine ever having the need for this—or ever doing this for our precious child.

It was described to me like this: "If you have an underground oil well fire and nothing will put it out, explosives greater than the fire itself are fed into the flames with the chance it will blow the fire to smithereens."

This is the same kind of medicine that surged through

Kim's veins to try and extinguish the fire of MS raging inside her body. It was a great risk, but there seemed to be no other alternative.

THE COSTS WERE MOUNTING

Every day she grew worse. However, at one point she seemed to improve slightly, yet a couple of months later her condition was so severe it felt like we were at the hospital every other day.

Kim continued to hemorrhage from the nose and the doctor would have to cauterize the blood vessels, then send her home. Again, we were with her 24 hours a day. She was so weak she could hardly lift her head off the pillow.

Finally the hospitals were reluctant to treat her any longer because she had no insurance. She needed quality treatment, but was too sick to wait in long lines at a community clinic. Plus, she would not have the same doctors treat her each time. It was too much of a risk.

Frank and I decided to refinance our home and pay what we could. We did this, but the medical bills were mounting daily.

A CALL TO JEDDAH

One Sunday night we had prepared dinner, but Kim was so sick in her bed that she couldn't eat. Tom was sitting in the chair next to her while Frank and I were in the family room watching television.

It was the lowest point in our lives,
but we were all together.

Suddenly there was a news flash: WAR IN KUWAIT!

The invasion started on August 2, 1990, and within two days of intense <u>combat</u>, most of the Kuwaiti Armed Forces were either overrun by the Iraqi Republican Guard or escaped to neighboring Saudi Arabia and Bahrain. The Emir of Kuwait, Jaber Al-Ahmad Al-Jaber Al-Sabah had already fled into the Saudi desert.

The enemy had bombed Kuwait and the palace had been destroyed. Their oil wells were on fire and the damage was devastating.

On television, for only a few seconds, they showed a panoramic picture of the Emir of Kuwait and his associates. They were seated around a large table in a conference room at a hotel. As they panned the faces of the group, suddenly I shouted to Frank, "That is where our help is going to come from!"

He could hardly comprehend what I was talking about. Then I said, "If I only knew where they were."

Frank responded, "I know. I saw exactly where that video was taken."

I questioned him, "How do you know? He quickly told me that he saw a matchbook on the table as the camera panned the group. "They're at the Sheraton Hotel in Jeddah, Saudi Arabia."

Immediately, I ran into the bedroom and said, "Kim, you must get up. Get dressed and come into the kitchen. I know that God has shown me where our financial help will come from."

I picked up the kitchen phone, dialed the overseas operator and asked for the Sheraton Hotel in Jeddah, Saudia Arabia. By this time Kim was in the wheelchair and Tom was pushing her into the kitchen.

"MAY I PLEASE SPEAK TO THE EMIR?"

None of us knew what in the world we were doing—but we were on a mission and we needed help. We had practically exhausted our finances to have our daughter taken care of by the doctors at the hospital.

In my heart of hearts I knew God was speaking to me. I had to stay focused on Him and listen to His leading.

I told Kim, "Honey, when we get the Emir on the phone, you must tell him what you are going through and ask for his help." Without hesitation she agreed.

By this time the operator had connected to the hotel Frank told us about. The voice on the other end answered, "Ahlo, Sheraton Jeddah."

I replied, "This is Joan Gieson and Kim Gieson Lilley from the United States of America, and we are calling to talk to the Emir of Kuwait."

"One moment please," click, click click.

"Ahlo," someone answered! I said "May I please speak to the Emir?"

"This is the Emir. How can I help you?"

Immediately I explained, "This is Joan Gieson and Kim Gieson Lilley from the United States of America and we have a story to tell you. I introduced him to Kim and she started talking.

DESTROYED AND DEVASTATED

She gave her age and told him she was watching what was happening to him and Kuwait. She continued, "One day your country was doing very well, and the next it was being destroyed."

Then Kim told him that she, too, was experiencing the same kind of devastation. "The day of my wedding everything was perfect, but within 24 hours my body was attacked with sickness and now I cannot take care of myself. "

She also didn't hesitate to let the Emir know that she had no hospitalization insurance and no money for special care or medicine.

Without a moment's hesitation, he uttered these amazing words: "WE WILL HELP YOU, KIM."

He turned the phone over to his cousin, the Crown Prince, Sheik Saad Al Abdullah Al Sabah. He talked with her at length and then he asked her to repeat her story to the Minister of Health, Dr. Raymon Alawadi.

There were many calls in the next few weeks and we talked with him about our situation. He was so caring. We even were in communication with him when he traveled to Geneva for meetings and to other locations. He put us in touch with the Ambassador of Kuwait at their embassy in Washington, D.C.

HAPPY, BUT WORRIED

By this time, days, weeks, and months passed by. We knew God was going to work it all out.

Meanwhile, the doctors in St. Louis wanted to give Kim blood transfusions and administer other tests, but before allowing additional procedures, I asked the nurses to cover her stomach with a lead shield. They asked me why I was so persistent and I reminded them she was a married woman and may be pregnant. We had to make sure she was not putting herself in any more danger than she already was. They assured me that the gynecologist had tested her and she was not pregnant. Nevertheless, I insisted they protect her with the shield, "just in case."

The X-rays and tests were given and another doctor called the next day to ask Kim to come in for a visit, which she did. This physician was a woman gynecologist.

A day later she called Kim and asked that she and her husband come to the office. Frank and I tagged along. We all sat in the waiting room, then Kim and Tommy were called in to see the doctor.

When they walked out, they shouted, "We are pregnant. We're going to have a baby!" They learned that Kim was already six months pregnant and no one knew it. She was going to have a girl.

We were happy but extremely worried.

When we phoned our new friend, Dr. Alawadi, the Kuwaiti Minister of Health, and told him our daughter was pregnant, he was very concerned. In fact, he called several times promising they would help.

We turned the entire situation over to God. There was nothing more we could do.

An Abortion?

Several weeks later the gynecologist called and said she had made an appointment with a genetic specialist since there were some concerns. Two days later we were back at the hospital with a new doctor. He examined Kim, administered several tests, then called both of us to his office where we received some frightening news.

He explained that the medicine she had taken for the MS, plus all the tests, procedures, and bleeding during the prior months were damaging to the baby. What he said next was far worse. "The baby will be born with a cleft palate, club feet, and be brain dead." Then he turned to Kim and told her, "It is my recommendation that you have an abortion and I will help to arrange it."

I asked, "Sir, can you do anything to change this."

"Nothing," he sadly responded.

"How much do we owe you?" I wanted to know.

He gave the amount and I wrote out a check from our near-depleted account. Then I turned to Kim, smiled, and said, "Let's go home and paint the room pink!"

We did just that. Pink curtains. Pink bows. Pink blankets. Pink dresses. Pink everything!

———————— *·* ————————

By this time she was seven months pregnant
and we were getting ready for a baby girl.

We continued to talk frequently with the people from Kuwait.

WOULD THERE BE PROBLEMS?

Finally, the moment came when Kim announced, "I think we'd better get to the hospital quick."

The family went with her and we were all praying—plus there were many others who were interceding on her behalf. We filled the waiting room.

The doctors did not understand Kim's decision to go through with the delivery and were thinking the worst. But God had other plans.

Out the baby popped with her eyes wide open to greet the world!

The doctor called for the neo-natal staff and in ran a group of nurses and medical assistants. The baby was whisked away and placed in an incubator. They suctioned her nose and throat, then took her to the critical care unit.

Kim and Tom were only able to catch a glimpse of her before she was taken away. They saw the most beautiful, healthy baby girl. No parts missing; nothing wrong with her in any way. Both feet and legs straight as arrows and a twinkle in her eyes just like her mom's.   September 29. What a great day that was. Our first grandchild was born and she was perfect in every way.

Kuwait was keeping in touch with us. It was the middle of the night because of the time difference and they seemed so delighted to hear the news about the baby and wanted to know all the details.

----

*Kim and Tom named their daughter Joan—
after me. What an incredible honor this was.*

In a few days the baby and Kimmy came home but it wasn't long until Kim was sicker than ever. By New Year's Eve she was back in the hospital and started the same five-day treatment I mentioned earlier. She came home in a week but was really no better.

For the next few months, I had the privilege of taking care of Kim and Joanie. And Tom was such a tremendous help.

A Life-Changing Announcement

It was an early spring morning, about 5:00 A.M., and I was getting the baby ready for Kim to nurse. When I went into the room, my daughter said, "Mom, I can't see her very well. Tell me, what does she really look like?"

My heart was breaking at the thought my daughter couldn't see her own baby. I replied, "She is the most beautiful child I have ever seen." I took Kim's hand and had her touch and trace Joanie's face. I told her, "She has the most gorgeous blue eyes—just like her father. And the face of an angel, just like you."

In the background, all of a sudden I heard a sound coming from our television set. Someone announced, "This is your day for a miracle." And I heard music—the same music they played at the Kathryn Kuhlman services years earlier.

I turned to Kimmy and excused myself. "Hold on tight to Joanie. I'll be right back."

What I was watching came from the Benny Hinn Ministry in Orlando, Florida. And they announced there would be a Miracle Service in Chicago in one week.

I ran back into Kim's room and told her, with great excitement, "There's going to be a Miracle Service in Chicago in a few days. I'm going to charter a bus and take you and your wheelchair—and all the sick people I know. I believe God will heal you."

We did just that. We got the bus organized, left the baby at home in the competent hands of grandpa, and took off for Chicago.

SPECIAL SEATS DOWN FRONT

Kim was very sick when we arrived, but the services did not start until the next night. After a full day's rest, she mustered enough strength to get back on the bus and head for the auditorium.

The streets were filled with buses and people were everywhere. When the doors opened, there were about 20,000 people waiting to get inside. Fortunately we found a seat before they had to lock the doors and turn people away. I got Kim settled, but she could not see the stage. One of the ladies from our group, Arden Welch, came back to us and said she knew people in the ministry and they had given her two seats down front. She gladly offered them to Kim and Tom. But Kim's wheelchair had to be moved to another location.

I stayed with the two of them until an usher asked me to move. I walked off to the side, but kept my eyes glued on my daughter.

Being there reminded me so much of the work I had done for Kathryn Kuhlman. I would hear God speak to me, "That lady there is being healed," and "That child in the blue dress is receiving a miracle."

The gift given then was still in operation.

The person next to Kim had moved to another seat, so I sat down and was grateful to be by her side.

"WHAT'S HAPPENING TO YOU?"

I remember giving this analogy to my daughter. "Honey, if you need bread you must go to the bread store. You cannot find it in a place that doesn't sell bread. And if you need a mighty miracle you must go where God's presence is—and baby we are here. He is present in every inch of this building. He is here and you have come to receive your miracle."

All of a sudden I felt my Kimmy was being healed. I turned to her and asked, "Kim, get up and do something you could not do before."

She rose to her feet and, amazingly, she had regained her

balance. Her vision was back to normal. She could now feel her legs and her stomach, which she had lost the feeling in more than a year before. She could hold her own arms straight up.

She moved into the aisle and started to walk—which prior to the service she couldn't do alone.

She walked. And then she ran!

Pastor Dave Palmquist saw what was going on and rushed up to her. "What is happening to you?" he wanted to know.

Kim, through her tears of joy, told him, "I was diagnosed with MS and couldn't do all this moments ago."

He talked with her for a few minutes, then brought her up to the top step of the stage. My heart was leaping out of my chest as they stood there for a while, waiting for Pastor Hinn to see them. But when he had finished with the person on the other side of the stage it seemed like he was ending the service.

Then, all of a sudden he looked over at Kim and asked, "What is happening over there?"

She ran up to him and explained all she had gone through for several years, "And now it's all over."

She could see. She could walk, She could turn in circles, touch her nose with her eyes closed, and so much more. Hallelujah!

BREAKING THE CHAIN

The service came to a close with my beautiful child being healed and Pastor Benny kneeling by her side, praising the

Lord together with 20,000 other people.

Before we left St. Louis I had shirts made for everyone on our bus that read, "Father, we have come for our Miracle"—and, praise the Lord, that's what Kim received.

My daughter told Pastor Benny her mom had brought a busload, so he asked me to come up on the platform.

This almost didn't happen. I was wearing a sweatshirt, and part of the decoration was a chain hanging across one shoulder and down under the arm. When I moved to stand up, the chain became caught on the chair and I couldn't pry it loose. When I started walking, I almost pulled the entire eighth row with me! Chairs were clanging and I nearly lost it. Finally, the person behind me broke the chain and I ran up on stage.

Once there, I could hardly speak, but managed to mutter a few words.

AN UNEXPECTED INVITATION

After the service was over, several of the assistants in the ministry came over to me and said, "Pastor Benny would like to see you."

I went with them to his dressing room and his words to me were: "My staff and I have been praying for someone to help me in the services for two and a half years—and I believe the Holy Spirit told me you were the one."

That invitation was in 1992 and I have had the privilege of working with his ministry ever since, except for a short period. And I pray I will continue to do so until the Lord has other plans or takes me home.

This has been a real call on my life and I always want to be faithful to what the Lord has ordained.

―――――――― ✍ ――――――――

God knows where we are at all times and we must
be ready to move when He gives the orders.

By the way, we called the wonderful folks in Kuwait and told them we did not need their help after all because, "Our God has just healed Kimmy."

They did not understand, but were very happy for us. Every year, we receive a Christmas card from Dr Alawadi, always wishing us well.

As we look back, those we met who were diagnosed with MS at the time of Kim's illness have passed away, but God had a different plan for her life. We will forever be grateful and give Him all the praise and glory.

I HANDED HIM THE PHONE

Several years later, I heard Pastor Benny mention from the platform that he would love to go to Kuwait. I smiled inside, thinking, "If he's serious, I know the Big Guy. I have connections there and can arrange an introduction."

I waited quite a while before sharing with him the story you have just read. I needed to get a green light from the Lord.

One day, I asked, "Pastor, do you really want to go to Kuwait?" He said "yes," and I told him the whole story.

When I finished, he got up and walked away without saying a word. But that night in a Miracle Service in Texas, he told the audience, "Today, Joan Gieson told me the most unbelievable story. At first I didn't believe it, but the Holy Spirit let me know it was the truth."

Then he asked me to share the account with the huge

crowed gathered in the arena.

Shortly thereafter, during a pastors meeting in a Florida hotel, I felt led to call Dr. Alawadi from a telephone booth and handed the phone to Pastor Hinn.

After I introduced them to each other, they talked for quite a while in Arabic, with the Kuwaiti doctor recounting the same story.

As I write this, our granddaughter, Joanie, is 18 years old and beautiful inside and out. She travels with me from time to time, praying for the sick and seeing God perform wonders. She has a younger brother who is also a tremendous blessing. He, too, helps me in the miracle services. He is 14 years old, 6'3" tall and wants to be a bodyguard.

Kim and Tom have been married for over two decades. They love the Lord and Kim helps me in the ministry we have in St. Louis. She and her brother, Michael, remain the best of friends.

If the Lord can perform such a wondrous work in our family, just think what He can do in yours. Trust, believe, and receive your miracle!

Twelve

"Happy Holidays, Prairie Farms Dairy"

And my God shall supply all your need
according to His riches in glory by Christ Jesus.

– Philippians 4:19

*H*elping the needy and homeless get through their lean and hard times has turned into a year-around labor of love for our family and ministry. The need is tremendous in the greater St. Louis area—and there is so much the people are desperate for:

- Diapers, formula, food, shoes, clothes.
- Money to help bury a loved one.
- A bus ticket to get to work or to return to their families.
- Help with children's school supplies.
- A safe place to hide from an abusive husband or boyfriend.
- Homes for neglected children.

The response of our ministry has been to help however we can.

Each year before the huge Christmas Dinner we provide for

the community, I make three wish lists. The first is my ultimate dream for each guest—a meal with every holiday treat they could think of, toys for each child, gifts for the adults, enough food to take home that would last them for a long time, plus a Bible.

My second list is for a little less. A good meal for every child, toys for the kids, a Bible, and at least some basic food to take home to tide them over.

The third list would be sandwiches, a salad, a piece of cake, and toys.

In the 50 years we have been providing our Christmas Dinners, our Father in heaven has always allowed us to reach our number one goal. There have been countless generous, caring people who provide in abundance, with enough left over to fill many food pantries in the area so others can be blessed.

One December, about 15 years ago, as I was checking my list, I realized we didn't have one toy to give to the children. I also thought perhaps a gallon of fresh milk for each family would be a wonderful addition to those little cartons of milk and ice cream we serve at the dinner.

I began to pray, "Please, Lord, bring in the toys and the gallons of milk. It would be such a treat for these kids."

Since I didn't hear one way or the other, I began thanking God in advance for the answer to my prayer. I even checked with the principal of the school we were using for the event to see if there was enough refrigerator space. He assured me, "I'll look into it."

I WAS STUNNED!

At the school, I was talking to God about the entire dinner when a man walked in and announced, "I have a 28-foot refrigerated truck outside if you have a need for it." I was stunned!

Then he added, "The generator runs on either fuel or electricity. The tank is full and I found an electric plug outside, so it's ready to go. You can even turn down the temperature and use it as a freezer."

Then he asked, "Do you have anyone with a CDL (Commercial Driver's License) who could drive the truck legally if needed? We had several, including my husband, Frank.

As the gentleman was leaving, the principal came running down the steps to inform me he had talked to the cooks and the maintenance department and they only had a limited amount of refrigerator and freezer space as most of it was being used by the school.

"Don't worry," I happily replied. "It's already taken care of." And I told him about the truck.

By this time my heart and brain were racing fast.
What was my Father in heaven up to?

I Dialed the Number

In a hurry, I found a *Yellow Pages* directory and turned to "Dairies." As I scanned through the list, I prayed, "Father, give me great favor with this call. Let whoever answers understand our need. Please put the right words in my mouth. Thank You, Father, for this milk and ice cream."

One company looked familiar as I always purchased their products for my family. So I picked up the phone and dialed the number.

It was about 6:00 P.M. on Christmas Eve. I waited for

someone to answer—and sure enough, they did. "Happy Holidays, Prairie Farms Dairy," a man said.

For a second I was startled. It wasn't a recording, but a real person! I shouldn't have been so surprised, after all, this is what I prayed for.

"This is Joan Gieson in St. Louis," I began, "Please write my number down in case we get disconnected." He did—and even read the number back to me. Then I shared with him the passion of our ministry—about our Christmas Dinner and how we feed thousands of homeless and needy individuals every year. "We are just a family with no resources, but we desperately need 10,000 small cartons of milk for the people to enjoy with their dinner and 2,000 gallons of milk for the families to take home."

Then I told him, "I really believe God has directed me to call your dairy and that you will help."

I heard the biggest laugh at the end of the phone.

"Please don't hang up," I begged him. "I believe God wants to use your company in this way and He will bless you beyond measure."

"Lady, you must be crazy," the man exclaimed. "You are not even a customer of our dairy. I really don't have time for this."

Trying to get in one last word, I told him, "Don't miss out on the blessing God has planned for you. Call me the minute you know you can help."

I heard the phone click—and he was gone. But I also knew he had my number and believed with every fiber of my being he would call back. I knew in my heart if God had someone working on Christmas Eve, He was going to do something spectacular. I asked Him to forgive me for that moment I doubted no one would be there to take my call.

OVER THE RIVER

Less than an hour went by before the phone rang. In a very gruff voice, I heard, "Is this Joan Gieson?"

"Yes," I answered quickly.

"I will have your milk ready for you, but we cannot deliver it. You will have to be here in 30 minutes." He gave us the address across the Mississippi river in Illinois and added, " You must guarantee us proper refrigerator temperature and return all the containers that hold the cartons of milk."

I was so excited to tell him, "You'll never believe this, but we have a 28-foot refrigerator truck parked at our door waiting for our use."

Frank jumped into the truck and away he went, following the directions given—over the river, across a dozen railroad tracks, to Prairie Farms Dairy distribution center. He drove through the gates and headed for the loading dock just as he was told.

The man saw Frank coming and the doors of the warehouse opened for him. A conveyor belt was turned on and suddenly three workmen came out to help Frank load the truck.

What I prayed for was there. Ten thousand half-pint milk cartons—white and chocolate. Plus all the gallons of milk we needed for the families.

"I WANT TO GET IN ON THIS"

However, when the truck was loaded, the concerned men

asked, "Don't you have bungee cords to tie this load down?"

When Frank said, "No," they replied, "Don't worry. We'll find you some."

They phoned a person at a nearby warehouse—and when they explained what they needed and what they would be used for, a huge Christmas Dinner for the needy, the man's heart was touched. He quickly responded, "I want to get in on this. What else do they need?"

The dairy man didn't know, but said, "This fellow will tell you when he comes over for the bungee cords."

Frank shared with him how we still needed toys for the kids.

"Come with me," was the response. And they went over to the Burger King warehouse. The foreman donated 10,000 novelty ice creams and thousands of small toys for the children—the kind included in kid's meals.

What generosity. What neat gifts—but God is God!

When Frank returned to the school, the volunteers who were setting up the dinner started yelling and high-fiving one another. Nearly everything we had prayed for was provided—except for the large toys we always love to give.

The party began on Christmas morning and the helpers were working on the last minute details. It was now 8:00 A.M. and the only toys we had were the small items from Burger King.

Seated at my desk, I looked up to heaven and said, "Jesus, it is Christmas. Your birthday. There's just got to be more for the kids."

At these dinners, we always share the miracle birth of Jesus, but we also want to demonstrate His love in a tangible way.

UNBELIEVABLE!

About that time, I saw a man walking through the back door. Before I could open my mouth, he said, "I'm a truck driver. I just stopped by to see if you need me to pick up anything for you at the last minute."

At that moment the telephone rang and I motioned for the driver to wait just one moment.

On the other end of the line I heard, "Ma'am, I know that you are in need of toys. Can you get a truck to this address in 20 minutes?"

Absolutely overjoyed, I replied, "I have a truck and driver just standing in front of me at this very moment. It will only take him ten minutes."

"Well, if you can get here soon, I'll give you as much as you need."

It was unbelievable! The man donated 20,000 toys! Some of them were remote control cars and airplanes. There were Barbie doll sets for the girls. Everything was brand new in their original boxes. Big, beautiful, fabulous toys! The dream of every child at Christmas.

From that first call to Prairie Farms Dairy, each year they have generously sent a huge tractor trailer loaded with milk, cottage cheese, sour cream, cream cheese, butter, and many varieties of ice cream. How neat is that!

I never have to question or imagine how wonderful and faithful our God really is. I've seen His love and abundance with my own eyes—over and over again. What a glorious testimony of our Father's love.

Thirteen

THE INHERITANCE

*The Spirit Himself bears witness
with our spirit that we are children of God,
and if children, then heirs—heirs of God
and joint heirs with Christ.*

– ROMANS 8:16-17

One day, returning home from a mission trip to the Holy Land, I called my dad from the airport in New York City. I was exhausted, but I wanted to see and talk to my father, whom I adored.

"Dad, I'll be in St. Louis in just a few hours. Frank is going to pick me up and we would like you to join us for dinner." He was delighted. I also phoned our children and asked them to join us as well.

We met at a little Italian restaurant not far from where we live—one we visit frequently.

I hugged and kissed my dad when I saw him. Salvatore Palermo meant everything to me. We talked for hours and the love of God permeated our conversation. I was so happy to be home with my family.

As we walked out of the restaurant, my dad leaned over and picked up our little granddaughter, Joanie, to kiss her goodbye. When he did, I heard an audible groan from him. Instantly, I asked, "Dad, is there something wrong? Did you have a pain?"

"Oh, no," he responded," Just gittin' old."

He hugged Joanie, got into his car and drove away.

"YOUR DAD NEEDS YOU"

The next day I slept later than usual, tired after the long flight home. Then, about 9:00 A.M., the phone rang. When I answered, a man said, "This is the Normandy Police. Come quickly. Your dad needs you." Normandy is a suburb of St. Louis.

I screamed for Frank to get dressed in a hurry and we rushed to the address the policeman gave us. We phoned our daughter and she was also on her way.

There was the fire department, the police, and my dad's car parked at the curb. I could see him slumped behind the steering wheel.

As I jumped out of our car, two firemen said, "Mrs. Gieson, he is gone. There is nothing you can do. Just stay here."

"But he is my dad," I pleaded. "I want to be with him. Please let me through." I needed more time with my dad. I needed his strength and his guidance. "Please, Father God, not yet—please!"

Once again, they protested, but I was determined. I remembered several times in our ministry when I laid hands on a person who had been pronounced dead, and by God's grace, they recovered and started breathing again.

Quickly, I ran to my dad. I rubbed his arm that had been so full of strength and said, "Dad, Jesus is here." His arm and hand had that beautiful Italian dark skin, and full of muscle. He had a full head of white hair—and hadn't lost one strand of it, even at the age of eighty.

Then I got down on my knees in the street alongside his car and began calling on the name of Jesus to bring him back. I rebuked death and prayed for the spirit of life to enter him. I called on Jesus to turn the situation around. I looked up to heaven and screamed, "Jesus, help us."

It seemed I was there forever doing everything I could and trusting my Father in heaven to turn it around, but there was no response.

All of a sudden I felt the pebbles on the street digging into my knees and I knew it was time to get up.

He was gone. God had called him home. Jesus was standing at the car when he got in and He said, "Come on Tutz—I'm taking you home"—and my dad dropped everything and joyfully went.

I walked around to the other side of the car. When I got in, I picked up his hand and held it tightly. I rubbed his arm and it was warm, just as always. I told him how much he meant to my life and how much I loved him. But he already knew how I felt—because I told him nearly every day.

By this time my husband and our daughter had climbed into the back seat of the car and we began to sing: *"Jesus loves me, this I know, for the Bible tells me so."*

We could feel the glory of God all around us and I was so grateful to have grown up with the greatest dad in the world.

SOMETHING I NEEDED TO KNOW

I knew I had to say goodbye, but I so appreciated those last moments holding his hand. About two hours went by and all of a sudden I saw the car coming to take my dad away. We got out of the car and sat on the lawn and we watched the car drive him to a funeral home. I just sat there quietly and remembered what he told me to do when this day came.

The year before, he had given me a key that was different than any other I had—and he had tied a red ribbon through the hole at the top of it. I recalled the time he told me, "One day, I want to tell you something you need to know."

He instructed me, "When I am gone, go to Boatmen's Bank, walk through the lobby until you come to the stairs. At the bottom you will see a lady behind her desk. Tell her you are Joan Gieson, Salvatore Palermo's daughter, and you have the key—and you need her help." I was crying so hard I could hardly breathe, but I had to do what my dad told me to.

I did just what he instructed. The woman, Mary Ann, was sitting there just as he described. She took my key, plus another one from a drawer, and said, "Follow me."

We went through a big round heavy steel door and the room was filled with nothing but small drawers. Some were larger than others. She stopped at one, put both keys into the lock on the box door, pulled the drawer out of the cubbie hole, and told me, "Open your arms. I will let you carry this to another room."

Having never been in a vault like this before, I followed her instructions completely. I placed the box on the table. She walked out of the room and gently shut the door.

I slowly opened the box and began to cry uncontrollable, not even knowing what I was about to find. I couldn't believe this was happening, yet I knew it was real. "I want my dad back, Jesus. I want him back."

THE KEY TO EVERYTHING

Inside the box was a piece of lined notebook paper. I carefully opened the folded letter and began to read: "I, Salvatore Rocco Palermo, leave to my daughter Joan Beverly Gieson every possession I have. This includes my house, my furniture, my car, my personal belongings, and every earthly thing I own. I withhold nothing from her. She is the heir to my entire estate."

Suddenly, the parallel between my earthly father and my heavenly Father flashed before me. Excited, I whispered, "I understand, Father God. I understand. Praise You, Jesus."

I understood that I am the heir of my heavenly Father's estate. *"And now that you belong to Christ, you are the true children of Abraham. You are his heirs, and God's promise to Abraham belongs to you"* (Galatians 3:29 NLT).

Scripture also tells us, *"But when the right time came, God sent his Son, born of a woman, subject to the law. God sent him to buy freedom for us who were slaves to the law, so that he could adopt us as his very own children. And because we are his children, God has sent the Spirit of his Son into our hearts, prompting us to call out, 'Abba, Father.' Now you are no longer a slave but God's own child. And since you are his child, God has made you his heir"* (Galatians 4:4-7 NLT).

---

*God has given me the key that unlocks
the door to everything He possesses.
Everything! Nothing is withheld.*

AN IMPORTANT LESSON

After finishing at the bank, I went to my dad's house, slipped the key he had given me into the lock, and opened the door. Because of his letter, everything there was mine. However, if I had *not* used the key I would have been unable to claim my inheritance. I would have benefited *nothing*.

Beloved, this had nothing to do with receiving monetary or material possessions my dad, Salvatore Rocco Palermo, had bequeathed me. In one split second I realized what my Father in heaven had made possible to me and to each one of us. My earthly dad taught me many life lessons, and he continued to do so even in his death. It was perhaps the most important lesson I ever learned.

My father, because of his love, left me everything. He withheld nothing. Every possession of his was now mine. At that moment, I could have protested, "No. This cannot be true. It must be for someone else. I am not worthy enough for this gift."

Thank God, I did not say any of those things. I was grateful for what he had done.

My father's estate was by no means lavish. It consisted of a 70-year-old 24x24 frame home that certainly wasn't worth much. His car was twelve years old and nothing in the house was of value to anyone but me.

Yes, I had inherited everything, but the real story is that I realized for the first time that my Father in heaven had given me everything in His Kingdom—if I would just believe and receive. *He had given me the key.*

It was a life-changing experience.

MY FATHER'S TRUE LOVE

A few days later, my father was ready for viewing at the funeral parlor. I put baskets of fruit, salami, cheese, Italian bread, olives, and red wine on the tables. Everyone ate until they were full. It was a celebration.

Over 1,000 guests showed up to show their respect and say goodbye to my dad—and almost everyone who passed the casket told me he was their best friend. Again and again I heard, "He always listened to me and was so interested in what I had to say." And, "I never heard him utter a negative word about anyone."

Maurice Sklar, the noted Christian violinist, flew in to play for the funeral. The last day of the viewing was now here. Every minute was so hard for me, knowing it was one minute less with my dad.

The day in his car when Jesus said, "Come home. Salvatore. It's time," he had been delivering food to an elderly blind lady who was not able to get to the market herself.

His friends cried, and so did I. At the age of 80, I still felt his life was cut too short. Yet, at the same time I was filled with the comfort of God's peace and joy.

The day of the funeral service, I conducted the eulogy. After all, who knew him better than me? I spoke of how my father's true love was Jesus, but how he loved his family also.

- How he saved my toe when I accidentally cut it off. How doctors said they could not put reattach it, but he insisted—not stopping at one hospital, but going to many, until he made it happen.
- How he managed to provide for us when we had nothing.

- How he taught us to ask and stand strong until we received.
- How to forgive and how to love everyone, no matter what.
- How to give more than we receive and to share.
- How to always be ready for a miracle coming our way.
- How to look beyond our circumstances and reach for the very best God has to offer—knowing absolutely nothing is impossible when God lives inside of you.

I gave an invitation to accept Christ and many came to the front of the chapel to give their hearts to the Lord.

What a celebration!

A husband and wife who were present, came up to me after the service and said, "We both work for AT&T, but after what we've heard today we have decided to go to our office and resign. We want to follow the calling of Jesus and make our lives count in service for God's Kingdom."

True to their word, they enrolled in a Bible School and are now serving on the mission field. I count them as part of my father's legacy.

Christmas came only a few months after my dad went to heaven and we hardly had to buy any presents. He had all the gifts ready for us in the basement of his house.

What an honor being his daughter, and as I've always said, "I want to grow up to be just like him."

BELIEVING PRECEDES RECEIVING

Not long after my father's home-going, we opened our Healing Rooms in St. Louis. This is a place where we pray for those with physical, spiritual, mental, or emotional needs. It is here that countless men, women, and young people have received their miracles.

One of the requirements for those who have been called to work in this ministry is that they must believe without question that everyone can be healed by God's power. *Everyone!* No ifs, buts, or maybes.

We must believe before we can receive. If I had not accepted the key, I would never have known of my father's wishes. His great gift would have gone by the wayside.

I trusted my dad's words, but I trust the Word of my Father in heaven even more. With joy, I receive His abundant inheritance.

Fourteen

QUILTS AT CHRISTMAS

*Trust in the Lord, and do good; dwell in
the land, and feed on His faithfulness. Delight
yourself also in the Lord, and He shall give you the
desires of your heart. Commit your way to the Lord,
trust also in Him, and He shall bring it to pass.*

– PSALM 37:3-5

*O*ne freezing winter morning, about five days before Christmas, as usual, my storehouse was running on empty. The only items we had were about ten small cans of string beans and a couple cans of sliced peaches.

On the other side of the coin, we had by this time approximately 13,000 hungry and needy people registered for our annual "Christmas Party"—a dinner for the underprivileged which was to be held at one of the largest public schools in St. Louis county. It is an event we have organized for the past 50 years.

We were all ready to go except for the fact that we had nothing to give the families to take home—no toys, no baskets of food. We had shared our need with those who could help, but at this late date there had been no response.

That morning when I got into my car to go to the office I started to pray for blankets for each person who came to the dinner, because it was so bitterly cold.

UNDER THE QUILTING FRAME

My mind raced back to my childhood, being with my grandma Gertie on Wednesdays at her church in Jennings, Missouri. The women in our family would go to the "quilting" meetings with other ladies from the church—regardless of the weather.

Before we would leave the house, Grandma Gertie would make each of us a peanut butter sandwich, wrap them in waxed paper, and add some potato chips and a piece of fruit.

As a small girl, I would sit under the quilting frame and eat my lunch.

The ladies gave me little scraps of fabric and I would make clothes for my dolls. I would thread the big needle and away I'd go. I kept all my sewing supplies in an old cigar box—which I left at church so it was always ready for me when I got there.

From my floor view, I watched the needles come through the big quilt and saw the pattern develop. I tried to imagine what the top was going to look like.

As they worked for their church, their country, and their families, I can still hear the women praying. I cannot begin to describe the love that went into the making of each of those quilts. They would eventually be given to a deserving person.

This was a precious time in my life—no worries, no complications, no struggles, no disappointments. It was a childhood memory I will never forget.

At the end of a very productive day we would catch the bus and return home.

"IS THIS THE PLACE THAT PRAYS?"

Now, many years later, I sat at my desk with my head in my hands, praying. This is my usual position when I'm calling on

God. What would we be able to give to the families at the Christmas Dinner?

The phone rang. It was one of about 200 calls that day. When I answered, a child on the line asked, "Is this the place that prays for everything?"

I answered, "According to the Word of God, we certainly do."

The child gave me his name and said, "My dog is gone. He's been missing for one week." Then he told me how much he loved his pet and wanted him back. They had looked everywhere, walked for miles searching for the animal, and had even placed an ad in the paper. "I'd really like him back before Christmas," he pleaded.

The boy had looked in the telephone directory under "Prayer" and found our number.

A grin came over my face when I thought about the two of us praying at the same time for such different things. His prayer was for a little dog, and mine was for a half-million pounds of food and toys. And each needed to be answered by Christmas—just five days away.

I thought about that kid having all the faith in the world, but knew he desired someone to pray with him—and was specific about what he wanted.

I asked him if he knew Jesus personally and he replied, "Yes, I do. And I go to church with my mom."

After I prayed with him for the dog to be found, he joined me with a loud "Amen."

After saying goodbye and putting down the phone, I sat there for a moment with a happy-to-the-heart smile.

WHO WOULD TAKE THE LOAD?

I was still seated there a few minutes later when the phone rang again. This time it was a truck driver in an 18-wheeler about three hours away from St. Louis. He told me, "I have 45,000 pounds of cargo on my truck and when I tried to deliver it, the load was refused."

He called the customer and they still didn't want the delivery.

The driver told his plight to an officer at a highway weigh station. The officer suggested he call his trucking company —and they too were stumped. He explained to them, "The officer here knows of a place he is sure will take the load."

The weigh station officer gave the truck driver the phone number of our ministry and he called me about the 45,000 pounds of goods. "Would you take it? " he asked.

"Yes," I shouted. I was so excited I could hardly get out our name and address. But neither of us had any idea what was in the truck.

I told him we didn't have a loading dock, but there was a tractor and trailer sitting in front of our office. "We can transfer the load from one trailer to the other."

"We'll have to do it quickly," he insisted. "You'll need about 10 men. I'll be there within two hours."

"WHAT ARE IN THE BOXES?"

I called a friend of ours, Mike Koeller, and he was happy to help and promised he would be at my place with his sons and their friends. He has faithfully assisted our ministry for years with large deliveries and has picked up tons of donations for our Christmas dinners from all over the country. He even got the great men and women of the union he belongs to,

Teamsters Local 600, to get involved and they loaned us skids, forklifts, tow motors, and pallet jacks, plus the men to operate them. He has been faithful whether it was 10 degrees below zero or 90 above. He never complained about the hours or asked for anything in return.

Mike, his wife Val, and their son Patrick became born again believers one Christmas day sitting around our dining room table, and he has never been the same. At one time he was a rootin'-tootin', cussing, drinking, gambling, mean guy. Now he is a Bible-carrying, devil-stomping believer who proclaims the Gospel of Jesus Christ.

------------ ✍ ------------

Mike never says "no"—and I don't either.
God always makes a way.

"The first time I met you I thought you were out of your mind," he told me. But he saw God at work, supplying every need.

Shortly after I talked to the truck driver who was bringing the load to us, Mike and his crew showed up. Even though it was freezing cold, when the truck arrived, they started transferring the cartons.

"What are in the boxes?" I wanted to know.

Mike and his men yelled back, "We don't know yet. When we finish, we'll open one and bring it to you."

I was so excited I could hardly wait. Then, when the trailer was unloaded, the driver came into our office and asked me to sign the paperwork saying the delivery had been received.

"What did you bring? I kept asking. He wasn't sure, but each box was carefully wrapped.

I ALMOST FAINTED!

I looked outside and the name of his truck line was *Genesis.* Why not? I asked him if he was a Christian, to which he answered "Yes" and told me the owner of the company was, too.

He was in a hurry to leave, but the men unloading the truck had told him about the big Christmas Dinner. He let them know he would be praying that we received everything we needed. He also told me, "If we get anything else that isn't accepted, I'll bring it to you."

With those words, the driver climbed into his truck and drove away.

About this time, Mike walked through the door and began opening one of the boxes. It was wrapped carefully and tied with brown, heavy string. He took his time opening the package, and when he pulled out the contents, I could hardly believe my eyes. It was a beautiful hand-made quilt.

I almost fainted. I grabbed onto it and clutched it to my heart. I cried and laughed, then Mike pulled out another one—and another, and another. Each was different and unique.

You should have seem me. I was screaming, jumping, praising God, and hugging Mike all at the same time!

By this time, the young men who were helping us carried in box after box. We opened them one by one and found hundreds of exquisite quilts. In fact, there were 45,000 pounds of them—absolutely gorgeous.

The labels on each box were a surprise to me. They had come from Lutheran churches all over southern Missouri. Can you imagine the emotions that were racing through my heart and soul?

AN EMAIL FROM IRAQ

That evening I went to church, and brought with me ten homeless people. Seated there, cozy and warm with my eyes closed, I was happy, secure, and savoring the delight of what had happened that day.

During the service, our pastor told the congregation about an email he had just received from a young man in our church named RJ, who was a soldier with our troops in Iraq. The email included how he was saved at the age of eight and after receiving Jesus, walked up to the pastor and said, "I'm going to have your job one day. I want to be a preacher."

The soldier wrote that he couldn't believe he was stationed in Iraq fighting for his country, but was so glad to be serving. Then he described going out into the fields to pick up wounded men and women who had been injured as they fought on the front lines. He wrote, "I would so much appreciate it if the church could send fabric that the rescue teams could sew together and make blankets to cover the wounded and get them to safety."

At that moment, my eyes were wide open. As the pastor continued reading the email, I began asking myself, "Is this what the quilts were lovingly made for?"

Immediately, I rose from my seat and started walking down the aisle to the front of the sanctuary. The pastor caught sight of me and asked, "Joan, what is it?"

"Pastor, did I hear the note from RJ correctly—that he wants fabric to make covers for the wounded?"

"Yes," that's correct," he responded.

"Well, today, I just received 45,000 pounds of handmade quilts, I will gladly give them to these brave soldiers."

With that, a lady in one of the front pews stood up and asked me to repeat what I had just said. So I did.

She began to cry, saying she was RJ's mom.

We hugged and embraced each other tightly. By this time the entire congregation was caught up in the spirit of the moment—and shouting praises to the Lord.

I gave her my name and our address and she said, "I'll be there tomorrow."

I arrived at the office early to open as many of the remaining boxes as possible so she could see the beautiful quilts. When RJ's mom drove up, the minute she entered the building we both cried again. And when she looked at the quilts our feelings were beyond words.

We packed as many boxes as we could cram into her car and she headed for the post office. It was just before Christmas and we knew the place would be crowded.

We had no idea how much the postage would cost.

The boxes were all taped and marked: IRAQ. SPECIAL DELIVERY. TO RJ FROM THE UNITED STATES OF AMERICA— and it gave his full name and Armed Service postal address.

A STRANGER'S QUESTION

Patiently, RJ's mom stood in line for a very long time trying to keep the boxes (which weighed hundreds of pounds) with her as she moved forward. When she finally reached the counter, the clerk asked, "Do you have the special form filled out to send these boxes to Iraq?"

No, she didn't, unaware one was needed. So, she went to another counter and began filling out the forms, then started the line process all over again. She was last in line when suddenly a woman walked up to her and asked, "Do you have packages to ship?"

Her answer was a definite "Yes." RJ's mom then proceeded to tell her what was being shipped—where it was going and why.

As unbelievable as it sounds, here is what this total stranger told RJ's mom. "I was sitting in my living room when I heard what I believed to be God telling me, 'Go to the post office quickly and you will find a person there who is mailing some very important packages. Pay the postage and you will be richly blessed.'"

The woman stood in line with the mother and paid hundreds of dollars to ship the quilts to Iraq.

When I learned what happened, I was humbled and fell to my knees to praise God.

From the depths of my heart I thanked Him for His love and how He watches over every step His children take.

RJ's childhood dream of being a preacher was being carried out on the front lines of Iraq. His congregation comprised of wounded soldiers—and I could see him offering comfort and sharing the love of Christ during the toughest moments of their lives.

Then I began thinking about the Lutheran women who had spent hundreds of hours making those quilts with such love and precision—praying over them and thinking about how they would bring comfort to some troubled soul.

My mind flashed back to my childhood, sitting under a quilting frame—listening to the women talk about what they would leave their families when they passed on, even talking of plans for their own funerals.

Now, years later, quilts were still being made in these

church circles. They had no idea that their handiwork would serve the highest calling in our land, assisting those who were shedding their life's blood so our country could stay free.

"WE FOUND HIM!"

On the day before Christmas, my thoughts were interrupted by the loud ringing of the telephone. It was the little boy who had called me about his lost dog.

"We found him! We found him!" the boy was yelling. He told me that his dog wasn't harmed in any way—and "he started wagging his tail as soon as he saw me. Thank you so much for praying."

Twenty-four hours later we served more than 13,000 people at our Christmas Dinner. The St. Louis County Police were on hand directing traffic.

Here's the exciting news. A total of 36 tractor trailers showed up, filled with such wonderful items. The total came to 1,650,000 pounds of food and toys. We fed every family and were able to give them large quantities of food for their pantries—fresh vegetables, fruit, meats, and canned goods. There were toys and games for the children, and each family received a new Bible.

You and I will never be able to out-give our heavenly Father. Nor will we know for sure how He is going to accomplish His purpose. One thing is certain: if we trust Him, He will perform the impossible.

Fifteen

MORE THAN MERE COINCIDENCE

*All things work together for good
to those who love God, to those who are
the called according to His purpose.*

– ROMANS 8:28

*I*n 1995 Pastor Benny Hinn held a Miracle Crusade in Rome, Italy. My husband, Frank, and I flew over a few days early to enjoy this magnificent, historical place. We roamed the ruins of the city, saw the hills, the beauty of the countryside, Vatican City, the shopping, the vineyards, and on and on. I could have stayed forever. I drank in the most beautiful art work and handmade items I had ever seen. I was in total awe the entire trip

Being Italian myself, I really felt at home—talking with my hands and having life centered around food! At first sight, the families seemed to be screaming at each other all the time, but in reality they weren't. This was just normal Italian talking. The more intense the conversation became the louder everyone spoke. Just as you thought a big fight was about to erupt, everyone would start laughing, lift their glass of wine, and hug and embrace one another. Now this is my kind of

Italian, and I laugh even as I think of it.

We walked for hours, wandering through the shops, eating at the sidewalk cafés, and trying to understand what in the world they were saying.

In our home, my grandmother and grandfather would not allow any of us to speak Italian because, settled in their new country, they would tell us, "We are Americans now, and we must speak American." The only time they broke out in their native tongue was when they became angry and used some choice, off–color words. Consequently, the little Italian vocabulary I picked up shouldn't be repeated!

Growing up in an Italian family I knew what it was to have everyone talk at the same time, yet no one missed a thing that was said. Oh, what fun we had!

Our journey to Rome was in the month of October, which is my birthday and my wedding anniversary, so I considered it special just to be there. I didn't get much sleep the whole time since there was so much to see and do and I didn't want to miss a thing.

During this trip, Pastor Hinn had a special audience with the Pope, who blessed us with a few rosaries. One of the team members, Ron Haus, kindly gave me one of the rosaries, and as you will see, this turned out to be a giant blessing for me personally.

A BROKEN FAMILY

Many years before this time, I had left the Catholic faith of my family. I became a born-again, spirit-filled Christian and was healed of a serious illness.

I was part of the ministry team of evangelist Kathryn Kuhlman. In addition, I was also attending prayer meetings, Bible studies, and worshiping God in churches all over the world.

My family thought I had lost my mind and was now a religious fanatic. As a result, they pulled away from me and I was no longer included in family gatherings and activities.

This was heartbreaking, but I could not, nor *would* I ever, change my beliefs.

------------&------------

I had found Jesus to be alive and more real to me than anyone or anything in this world.

Many years passed by and I was estranged from my family—showers, weddings, baptisms, visits, baking cookies together at Christmas time were sadly missed, especially those family gatherings.

My heart was heavy for a long time, but with God's help, I had to move on. I could not revert back to a dead religious belief. I had to stand true to my newfound faith. Jesus became my everything—my next breath, my friend, my brother, my Savior, my God, my Healer, my constant thought, and my risen Lord.

The Holy Spirit, my teacher and guide, was always with me, constantly protecting, giving wisdom, and filling me with new life. I knew that nothing was impossible because of Him. Wow! I am shouting Hallelujah even as I write these words.

WHAT AN AROMA!

In Rome, the night before the first Miracle Service, Frank and I walked to a little café to have dinner. I remember it being about 9:00 P.M. and the place was just coming alive. We were pulled in by the aroma of fresh bread baking, and as we followed our noses we came to a big brick oven inside the café filled with pizza and *focaccia* breads. I can't think of anything more appetizing!

Then we looked into the large glass meat and salad case and what we saw was like heaven to our hungry eyes and empty stomachs. Meats of all varieties, cheeses galore, olives, artichokes, peppers, to name just a few delights. The list goes on and on. I can smell it all over again. If you have never shopped in an Italian import store where they sell all these items, please do so. It is an unforgettable experience.

Frank and I spotted a table decked out with a bright red and white oilcloth. It was situated near the meat counter. A waiter approached us, ready to take our order, but we couldn't understand a word he was saying. So we stood up and pointed to the things we wanted. What a happy memory.

"I WONDER WHAT THAT IS?

As we sat there, the front door opened and in walked a woman who was a Sophia Loren look-alike. She was holding onto the leash of a small, hairy dog, who was excited about being inside where everything smelled so good. Accompanying her was a young man and woman.

My husband and I were surprised to see a dog permitted in a restaurant—but this was Rome! They came to the table next to us and sat down.

The inquisitive dog was now sniffing at my ankle and before long had wrapped his leash around the leg of my chair as well as my leg—and I was locked in. The two of us were hooked together and I could hardly stop from laughing.

The trio ordered their food and when it arrived, I noticed the man eating a dish I had never seen before. I turned to Frank and quietly said, "I wonder what that is?"

No sooner had the words left my mouth when the man cut a piece of his food with a fork, reached across the table and was ready to put it into my mouth!

I was shocked. First, a little dog had me chained to my chair and now a total stranger was feeding me! Instinctively, I opened my mouth and he popped the food in. How strange. But I chewed and swallowed and it was wonderful.

In his broken English, he then told me the name of what I had just eaten—and said he understood a little English.

His name was Alisso, and he introduced us to Momma Camellia and sister Giya, a precious family that lived just a few miles away.

---

*We talked for a long time and fell in love
with our new-found friends.*

AN UNEXPECTED INVITATION

Curious, they asked, "Why did you come to Rome?"

We told them about the Miracle Service that was scheduled the next day with Pastor Benny Hinn, but they did not understand. I still smile when I think of all the hand gestures we used trying to explain praying for the sick and how people's lives could be changed through a personal relationship with Jesus Christ.

It soon became very obvious that they wanted nothing to do with the church, with prayer, or even with the Pope.

As our hard-to-translate conversation continued, they related the story of how their Father left them when they were very young—abandoning them and their beautiful mother.

They went on to tell us their father was now supposed to be a Christian, but hoped they would never see him again.

As we talked, they begged us to come to their home the next day for dinner. We told them we couldn't but they insisted, saying they would come to the hotel, pick us up, and drive us later to the arena where the crusade was being held. Their invitation was so genuine and sincere, we finally agreed.

The next day, just as promised, Alisso arrived at the hotel at the appointed time. We learned later he had been there for hours to make sure he wouldn't miss us.

What a ride! He drove his little car like an Indy 500 racer! One hand stayed on the horn while the other held a long cigarette he puffed on non-stop.

LIKE A MOVIE SET

When we reached their apartment building and took the elevator to the 12th floor, we could already smell the same aroma as the café. Momma and Giya opened the door and it was like we were entering an Italian movie set. Plastic covered every stick of furniture. An old shawl was carefully draped on a chair and doilies adorned almost everything. These supposedly non-religious people had a crucifix hanging on practically every wall.

Flowers were growing in pots on the small porch off the kitchen, plus basil and oregano plants—and even a wheel-cranked clothes line strung across the courtyard between the apartment buildings. It was groaning with the day's washing.

If I were an artist, this would have been a perfect canvas to paint.

Momma had dinner prepared and ready for us and we asked if we could bless the food before we ate. I had never tasted anything so good in my life.

We couldn't spend much time with our generous hosts because of the Miracle Service that evening. I asked the family to please come with us to the meeting but they refused. Then, when it was time to leave, I asked one more time—and directed my request to Momma Camellia.

She spoke to her son and he explained that she finally said "yes."

"WHAT ARE YOU HOLLERING ABOUT?"

The five of us jammed into the smallest car in Italy and went flying down the narrow streets. Again, Alisso was chain smoking and honking that horn!

As we approached the auditorium we could see a great crowd gathering. There were people scurrying in all directions, getting in line waiting for the doors to open.

I told Alisso we would need to drive to the rear of the building so we could enter through the stage door. But just as we turned the corner, he started screaming, "There he is! There he is! That no-good ***** and that no-good woman with him!"

"Alisso, calm down," I told him. "What are you hollering about?"

As we drove through the security gate, he stopped the car and started to cry. "That's my no-good father, his wife, and her son. They call themselves Christians. What is he doing here?"

By this time the car was at the stage door and I told everyone, "Quickly. We must go in." The family didn't want to, but I took them by their hands and said, "We're going in!"

Once inside, I asked Alisso if he would help me interpret the conversations as I spoke with those who were praying for their healing.

Actually, I didn't give him time to say "no." I led Momma Camellia and Giya to seats on the front row and took Alisso by the hand, asking him to tell me what the people were saying.

I prayed with those in need for about two hours and the time flew by.

A GREAT COMMOTION

The service started and Alisso sat next to his amazed mom and sister. The singing was tremendous and the huge crowd was praising the Lord with one united voice. Then came the moment when Pastor Benny began praying and calling out many illnesses that were being healed.

It was time for me to go up on the stage and announce what miracles of healing God had performed in the physical lives of many individuals. I walked over to Alisso, grabbed his hand and said, "Come up here with me. I cannot understand what they are saying."

Now on the platform, we started announcing what was taking place.

At that moment, on the right side of the arena, directly in front of Alisso and me, a large group started getting loud and crying, and the ushers had to quiet them down.

Let me explain the reason for the commotion. When Alisso walked up on the stage, this group of people recognized him and were so excited they couldn't contain themselves. It was the entire congregation of Alisso's step-brother's church. It's where the father and step-mother attended—and the son of the wife was the pastor! He was one of the ministers responsible for Benny Hinn being invited to Rome. This church had been fasting and praying for Alisso, his mom, and sister for years, asking God to save them and give them peace in their hearts to forgive.

Wow! What a Mighty God we serve. That night a family was totally reconciled. Alisso, Momma Camellia, and Giya received Christ as their personal Savior.

In His perfect timing, the Lord took Frank and me half way

around the world, led us to a charming restaurant, and had a little dog wrap his leash around my chair and leg just so we could meet Alisso and his family. We insisted on them going to a Miracle Service and the rest is history!

Alisso now travels to other cities and countries helping his step-brother win souls. His life is totally changed.

Our heavenly Father had it planned all along, for just the right day, and the right moment.

OVER AND ABOVE

You and I have the most awesome God, and He is our Father. I can't emphasize this enough because there are times we fail to realize that a father will do anything for his children.

Let me remind you what is written in God's Word. *"Now to Him Who, by (in consequence of) the [action of His] power that is at work within us, is able to [carry out His purpose and] do superabundantly, far over and above all that we [dare] ask or think [infinitely beyond our highest prayers, desires, thoughts, hopes, or dreams]"* (Ephesians 3:20 Amplified).

A ROSARY FOR AUNT BEA

Earlier, I mentioned the rosary that had been given to me by pastor Ron Haus—one that had been personally blessed by the Pope. The day this happened, even though we rarely spoke, I called my Aunt Bea in St. Louis to tell her I had the rosary and I would be home in several days and would bring it to her. She had been very sick, and I knew this would mean so much to her since she was a devout Catholic.

Once our feet touched U.S. soil, I called from the airport

telling her I would be by her side as quickly as I could. When I arrived, her only son, his wife and children were there to greet me. I walked in, kissed my wonderful Aunt Bea, and placed the rosary in her hands. She cried, kissed it, and clutched it to her heart as tears flowed down her cheeks. Everyone in the room was choking back tears.

We stayed a while and I had the wonderful privilege of sharing with my family about Jesus being the Savior, not a religion or a denomination. I explained that the place I worshiped was my preference, but Jesus was my everything.

The eyes of my relatives were fixed on the church —which was the reason they had separated themselves from me for all of those years.

AN UNEXPECTED RESPONSE

That night I tossed and turned remembering how good it was to see them, but the major focus was the rosary I had given to Aunt Bea. As I saw her clutching it so tightly, it was as if the rosary instantly became a savior to her.

The next morning I knew in my spirit the first thing I needed to do was phone her. It was so meaningful to talk with my aunt; it had been so long since I was able to break through that barrier. I told her how much I loved her and how much she meant to me.

We talked about the night before and how delighted I was to give her the rosary. I reminded her that as precious as it might be to her, no rosary in the world— even one blessed by the Pope—could ever get her to heaven.

She had been bed-ridden for a long time and the doctors were now saying they could do no more. Seizing the moment, I said, "Aunt Bea, the Word of God says if we are not born again we are not going to spend eternity with Him, and that only comes by inviting Christ into your heart and asking Him to forgive your sins."

I heard her getting upset on the other end of the phone, yet I knew this may be the only opportunity I would have to speak to her in this way. I could not leave her with the false impression a rosary was going to save her soul.

"Aunt Bea," I continued, "we can pray together right now and Jesus can instantly become your Savior and you will know you have followed what the Word of God says to do to ensure eternal life."

Nervous, and with a shaky voice, she repeated the sinner's prayer and repented of her sins. Together, we said "Amen" and thanked Him for life and forgiveness.

SHOCKED AND DELIGHTED

Then, in her own way, she asked, "Now I want you to promise me you will never tell anyone about this."

I assured her I would not mention it to another person unless God spoke to me and said it was okay. Then I repeated, "I love you," and hung up the phone.

From that time on I called many times and talked to Aunt Bea about how important she was to my life—but that she was much more important in God's eyes.

About a year later I was conducting services in Canada when the phone rang in my hotel room. I was surprised to hear my cousin on the other end of the line. He started to cry as he told me his mom, my Aunt Bea, had just passed away. Then he asked, "Would you come home and conduct the service for her in the chapel at the funeral parlor?"

I was shocked and delighted all at the same time. I answered, "Of course. I would be honored."

———————— 🖋 ————————

When I hung up the phone, I shouted
praises to the Lord. Only He could have
made something like this possible.

I tried to change my flight from Toronto, but no seats were available. So the funeral was postponed until I arrived.

A GLORIOUS DAY

The undertaker met me at the airport and took me directly to the funeral home. All the way he talked about the rosary I had given to her—I was not aware that anyone outside the family knew.

He led me into the room where my aunt was in repose. There she lay, lovely as ever, with the rosary draped through her fingers. I sat there and shared from my heart everything I wanted to say.

The next morning the chapel was packed with people—a huge crowd. I only knew some of them, but as the music started to play it was time to talk with her friends. On the way to the podium, my heavenly Father spoke to me: "Now is the time to tell everyone what you really know about your aunt." I began by asking those present, "How many of you are here because you loved my Aunt Bea?" Their heads nodded in agreement.

Then I added, "Would you like to see her again and be with her and her Savior forever? If so, raise your hand."

Hands shot up all across the room. Then I told them the story of the rosary and how she cherished it so much, but explained that it would never gain her entrance into heaven.

I shared the fact that, "One day she asked Jesus Christ to

come and live in her heart and He did. Now because of that life-changing decision, she was at home in heaven. And if we wanted to be with her again we would have to make the same commitment. How many want to follow in her footsteps and accept Christ?"

Everywhere, all across the chapel, people raised their hands. They repeated the sinner's prayer with me and became God's children.

What a glorious, memorable day—one I will never forget. I too look forward to spending an eternity with my Aunt Bea—and all those who have given their hearts to Christ.

A MASTER PLAN AND PURPOSE

All this unfolded because one day Pastor Benny invited my husband and I to go to Italy, not having a clue it was part of God's divine plan all the time. In Rome, an Italian family was saved—unaware that an entire community had been praying and fasting for them for years.

Then to think that a rosary blessed by the Pope opened the door for me to see my own family reunited—and this became a turning point for my aunt's story to be told, causing many others to accept Christ.

When we walk in God's will, He uses us to fulfill the plan He set into motion from the very beginning. We may not realize what He is doing until the miracle has already taken place.

Today, step out in faith and trust Him with all your heart. He will never let you down. Yes, the power that is at work within you is able to carry out His purpose—*"far over and above all we dare ask or think"* (Ephesians 3:20).

Sixteen

GOD SPECIALIZES IN THINGS THOUGHT IMPOSSIBLE

*I say to you, if you have faith as a mustard seed, you
will say to this mountain, "Move from here to there," and
it will move; and nothing will be impossible for you.*
– MATTHEW 17:20

Over the years I have personally witnessed hundreds—
even thousands—of miracles. I'm not talking about a person
suffering with a minor headache who suddenly felt better,
what I have seen defies medical explanation. All I know is that
the same power that raised Jesus from the dead is at work on
earth today.

Let me share a few testimonies of men, women, and
children whose lives have been touched by the healing power
of Christ. With Him, absolutely nothing is impossible!

The Lord of the Dance

Several years ago, a friend of ours in Florida named Mona
asked us to spend Easter with her and her family.

We were delighted to do so since I needed a little R&R from all the traveling I had been doing in the crusades around the world—and our family would enjoy the break.

We were seated around Mona's dining room table eating when the doorbell rang. When Mona went to see who it was, there stood a beautiful young woman named Kim—the same name as our own daughter. She was welcomed to join us.

A young man held her by the hand, walked her to the dining room, and helped her to a seat. She obviously could not see. He said, "I'll be back to pick you up in a few hours."

From that moment on, our wonderful Holy spirit took over.

ON THE AIR

When Kim was born, nearly 20 years earlier, she was two months premature. The doctors were able to save her life, but the oxygen given robbed her of her sight. Every year her vision grew darker and darker, until as a teen she was declared legally blind.

I learned that Kim had always loved music and on this day we heard the voice of an angel.

As we sat on the patio, she sang Amazing Grace. How beautiful and touching was her rendition.

At the time I had a half-hour radio program in St. Louis—which I originated from anyplace in the world. I went inside, connected to the station and began the broadcast. As the program unfolded, I began to share with my listeners the story of Kim. Then, during a song from a guest, I laid my hands on Kim and prayed that God would restore her sight. Something miraculous began to take place, even as the live radio program was in full swing.

With a heart of thanksgiving, we began to praise the Lord and let the listeners in on what was happening.

She Saw the Sand

After the broadcast, we went over to the piano and Kim began to sing—and actually read the words from the hymnal. This was something she had never done before. We sang "The Lord of the Dance" and all began to dance and rejoice. Kim was so excited. "I am going to stay up all night and look at the things I have never seen before."

All of a sudden there was a knock on the door. It was the young man who had dropped Kim off earlier. He was so surprised and thrilled that he screamed with delight. He could not contain himself and cried like a child, looking at Kim as she relished seeing everything after so many years.

We all made plans to go to the beach the next day. Kim had been there many times, and had felt the water, the hot sun beating down on her, and the sand trickling between her toes. But this day was different. Kim *saw* the blue waves. She *saw* the beige sand—and praised God because once she was blind, but now she could see!

Sitting on the beach, we watched Kim as she reveled in her newfound sight. She ran and played ball without anyone guiding her—and we were amazed as she stepped into the ocean all by herself.

What a joy and privilege it is to be a child of God and believe Him for what we have need of. All through this book I have been telling you what our God can do—if only you will allow Him to. Even in your darkest valley, He is the same yesterday, today, and will be forever.

She Couldn't Stop Running

I can still remember the day a woman named Betty Lou visited our Healing Rooms with a severe back condition that was the result of a horrible accidental fall.

In her own words, here is what happened:

On January 21, I was at my daughter's house, and when I started to get out of my chair I tripped over the chair leg. It sent me end over end and I hit the basement door. I slammed against the door and hit the floor very hard. It knocked the wind out of me and I was in terrible pain.

My daughter rushed me to the emergency room where they took X-rays which showed I had a fracture of the back. It was in my lumbar area near the spine. They gave me this big, hard plastic back brace to wear.

It was so uncomfortable, but I wore it anyway.

My orthopedic doctor informed me I would have to wear it probably at least until August. It usually takes a year for this kind of injury to completely heal.

"Heat Went Down My Back"

My friend, Alma told me about the St. Louis Healing Rooms. I called Joan Gieson on March 11 and she said, "Come on over. We would like to pray for you." When

I arrived, Joan reassured me, "You're going to be all right."

Two ladies laid hands on me and I felt good after their prayers, but didn't feel totally healed. I still experienced pain. So I sat in a chair and waited for my friend to finish her time of prayer.

Joan personally said, "I want to pray for you." So she did—lifting me up on her back—my feet weren't touching the floor. And as she prayed, HEAT surged down my back. Joan told me, "I believe you're going to throw that brace away and begin to run around the room." This is exactly what I did!

I ran and ran and I couldn't stop. I left the back brace at the St. Louis Healing Rooms. Hallelujah!

Jacob's Journey

No sickness or condition is too difficult for the Lord. Whether the problem is lung cancer or leukemia, hearing loss or heart disease, arthritis or asthma, He is the true Healer.

Allow me to share a letter we received from the father of an autistic boy named Jacob:

Our son was born with autism. Beyond the emotions and fears, I didn't know what the future would bring. However, my wife always had the faith that he was going to be okay. On several occasions, we were informed that our son would end up in an institution.

At five years old, Jacob entered into an autistic

children program where he spent the first two years of his education. He spent the next eight years in learning disabled classes where he gained many skills in areas of speech, fine motor skills and academic subjects.

We were introduced to a church where you spoke four years ago. At the end of the service you had a conversation with my son and told him, "Jesus saw you surrender. He knows your heart." Then you asked God's blessing to heal him and give him a long life. You asked that all his infirmities line up with the Word of God; that he may think correctly and learn—to become all the Lord wanted him to be.

We are still overwhelmed with joy. People ask us all the time, "What is your secret (for Jacob's success)?" We show them the video of the service. We still cry when we replay the tape. God has blessed us so much.

Recently, his high school principal submitted Jacob's name to the local newspaper as a potential story. The paper interviewed us and it was released. However, what was left out of the article was our total belief that our Lord Jesus Christ healed him. (We had even shown the reporter the video tape of the service).

We had always prayed for Jacob and we thanked God for what He would do in our son's life. Because all Jacob had and needed was Jesus.

Our son was moved into regular academic classes at the start of his sophomore year. He had to complete four years of English in his last two years of high school. In addition, he had to pass all the state's standards of learning (SOL's) to obtain a standard diploma at graduation.

SURROUNDED BY ANGELS

During the past two years Jacob obtained his driving license, managed a 3.81 grade point average, was elected Prom King, inducted into the National Honor Society, received two Honor Roll awards, and ranked 15 of 369 in his graduating class.

He plans to attend college this fall. This is a new chapter in his life and he is looking forward to the challenges ahead.

We are certain that Jacob is surrounded by angels. The teachers he had throughout school had uncommon valor. Many areas of his life opened up and God's mercy and grace flourished.

In the beginning stages of Jacob's journey, the world said he was worthless; a throwaway. What "they" didn't realize is that God made him, and in His perfect timing permitted Jacob to be a lesson to all those who have come in contact with him.

Most of all, the best is yet to come!

We count our blessings every day and understand that only the Lord directs our paths. We have also learned that too often we tell God all of our problems instead of telling our problems how big God really is!

A Divine "Halo" for Dave

*D*octors informed one young man, Dave ("Shorty")—who

had been involved in a motorcycle accident, that he had broken his neck and back. They told him that his injuries were very similar to those sustained by actor Christopher Reeve and that he would possibly have to wear a "halo" brace around his head, plus a back brace. He was scheduled for surgery a couple of days later and they let him know he would be in the hospital for at least three months.

A prayer team from the Healing Rooms was dispatched to the hospital and that evening both he and his girlfriend received Jesus as their personal Lord and Savior.

The team fervently prayed for Dave's healing. The next day, as the doctors read the latest MRI report, they commented on how something had changed in his back. They no longer saw a need for surgery.

Instead of undergoing an operation, Dave was released from the hospital. His injuries did not require a halo brace. God had a special "halo" reserved for him that was divine. Praise the Lord!

When he returned for additional tests, the X-rays proved there were no problems at all with his bones. "You can go back to work," they told him. He is a heavy equipment operator and mechanic.

What a complete turn-around from three weeks earlier when his future looked so bleak.

Wow! God is faithful to His Word and answers our prayers.

Sandy was Set Free

When you read the New Testament, you soon discover that Jesus not only performed physical healings, but had a ministry of deliverance.

In our Healing Rooms we have seen people set free from depression, condemnation, physical and emotional abuse, demonic forces, guilt from past behaviors, and so much more. This is a report we received from a woman named Sandy:

Not long ago, I was one step away from committing suicide. My husband and I were strung out on drugs. I had quit my job and we were about to lose our home. I felt like there was no hope for tomorrow.

I awoke early that morning, made some coffee, and decided to sit on our back porch and watch the sun come up.

For whatever reason, I had picked up a Bible; I thought perhaps I might gain some comfort in reading it.

After awhile, I began to pray for God to help me. As I read more, I started hearing a voice in my head telling me to walk up to the church on the corner. I thought it was just me, so I dismissed it at first. But I kept hearing the voice. Five times I heard, "Walk to the church on the corner," so at last I gave in. "Okay, I'll go."

With each step I remember being so scared and wondering, "What was I going to say to the preacher? That I was a drug addict? That I quit my job and was just waiting to be thrown out of my home? That I was an adulteress and my current husband was my third?"

A STILL SMALL VOICE

How could anyone forgive the things I had done? I

was not worthy of forgiveness. But this still small voice in my head kept repeating to me, "Be not afraid. He will meet you at the door." Over and over I kept hearing the voice, "Be not afraid. He will meet you at the door."

As I reached the church, I walked up to the back door and rang the bell. It was early and I wasn't sure anyone would be there that time of day. But as I pushed the bell a second time a man came down the stairs. I wanted to run but couldn't. It was as if I was stuck and afraid to move.

By the time the man reached the door I thought I was going to fall, I was so scared my knees were weak and I was shaking all over. On opening the door, he asked, "Can I help you?"

I told him I wanted to see the pastor. His response surprised me. "I am the pastor," he said. "Why don't you come in?"

As I followed him up the stairs to his office I said to myself, "How could this be happening just like the voice said it would?"

I spoke to the pastor for quite a while that morning, and before I left the church I had surrendered my life to the Lord.

I would like to tell you everything was all right from that day on, but all I can really say is that I have not been the same since. I have no longer wanted to do the things I had done in the past.

ABUSED AT SEVEN

Unfortunately, my home situation did not change

instantly. Probably like everyone, I thought God would miraculously change my life and make everything immediately okay. But that did not happen. The one aspect that changed was, me. I was still searching—but didn't know for what, or exactly how to find it. All I knew was God was calling me.

For over fifty years I carried around guilt and the feeling that I was not worthy of forgiveness. God could forgive everyone else, but I was so bad He would never pardon me.

I was sexually abused at the age of seven by a neighbor. I had a father who was not only an alcoholic, but was very cruel when he drank. He took his anger out on me because I always tried to protect my mom from his rage. I would stand in front of her and take her beatings instead of letting him take his wrath out on my mom. This would make him mad—and as I grew up, the beatings became worse.

As I recall it now, I don't think he liked how strong I was.

I was raped at fourteen and was told by my father, "You deserved what you got." He made me feel like I was no good. He would curse and call me ugly names.

That was the last straw. I couldn't take any more. From that time on I rebelled against the world. I felt as though no one loved me, so I ran away and began doing things I am now ashamed of. I drank, did drugs, and had sex with just about anyone I could. I cared nothing about my self-image. What happened in those days I have never and will never tell anyone but God.

RELEASED FROM BONDAGE

In the pastor's office, God wonderfully forgave me of all my sins, but I had to learn how to forgive myself.

I met some people at the church that first week who have helped carry me through some really rough spots. They pray with me, help me to learn God's Word, and show me how to apply it to my everyday living. They have become very good friends.

These same individuals have been volunteering at the St. Louis Healing Rooms and have taken me there with them.

The Lord has been dealing with me for some time regarding forgiveness—preparing me to be receptive to the things I would hear from His servants. One message in particular opened my eyes as to how much God wants us to be free, but we have to do our part and give up the baggage we still carry around. I learned how to give away and release what I had been harboring for so long.

Shortly thereafter, I was attending a class at the Healing Rooms of Joan Gieson's Ministries of Love. In the middle of the class, God started working on my heart. After the session I asked if I could be prayed for.

That night, God set me totally free from all the junk I had carried around for all those years.

———————— ✒ ————————

I have been released from a bondage I no longer have to accept. No longer do I feel unclean and dirty.

I just want everyone to know that no matter what you've done, no matter how bad you think you are or were, you too can be set totally free. All you have to do is honestly seek God with all your heart and believe that He sent His only Son "Jesus" to die on the cross for your sins. That through the blood of Christ you will have everlasting life.

Ask Him to forgive you and He will set you free. Give Him all the praise and glory, and put Him first in everything you do.

Praise God, He has set me FREE!

X-Rays Don't Lie

*W*hen Michael was born at St. Anthony's Hospital, all was fine until the next day, when nurses noticed that he was bloated and spitting up bile. Michael was taken to St. Johns Neonatal Intensive Care unit where doctors found that he had not yet passed his first bowel movement, which is called Meconium. To the doctors, this was a red flag that this child had cystic fibrosis. Michael would spend the next 12 days in the NIC unit before going home.

For the next 18 months Michael would battle pneumonia, pseudomonas and many lung infections. At times he was so weak that he would and could not eat. Michael was not crying. He just really didn't have the strength to fight and live.

It was at this point his parents brought Michael to our Healing Rooms in St. Louis. The tender hand of God reached down and touched this boy miraculously. Says the mother:

After Michael's healing, each time we would go to the clinic, the doctor's would listen to Michael's lungs by stethoscope and tell us they sounded clear as a bell. Michael had always been low in weight, but with each day that went by, I saw him eating, gaining weight, and thriving—something the doctors said wouldn't happen.

They told us Michael would not talk, but after the prayers for him at the Healing Rooms, now he does. Even at two years of age, he gives God all the glory. Our night time prayer with Michael includes him repeating with us "I am healed!"

The proof of Michael's healing was what a doctor said when he saw a new set of X-rays.

In September, Michael had a problem with his bowels and a new set of X-rays were taken. The condition was corrected, but in the process, my husband told the doctor that in the past Michael had pneumonia. This was amazing to the physician who was looking at the X-rays. "Where there should be scaring from pneumonia, there is none. Such scaring just doesn't go away on its own" he said.

Last week a nutritionist from the hospital called to see how Michael was doing. "Oh, he's just fine," I told her. Then, as she was about to hang up, she asked, "Is there anything I can do?"

"Yes," I answered. "I wish I could have Michael's X-rays."

"I don't think that's possible," she replied. "They stay with the hospital."

Well, a few days later there was a large envelope in our mail box with the words: "X-RAYS. DO NOT BEND."

I don't think this was by accident. It was as if God was telling us, "I want My hand to be seen."

Michael's father added, "The Healing Rooms and Michaels's healing have been a tremendous blessing, not only for him, but also for us.

Five Miracles for Bernadette

*W*e serve a God of abundance who gives us more than we can ask or think. This is certainly true for a woman named Bernadette. I will let her tell the story in her own words:

> *One of our pastors asked if I would work with a team of nurses in a First Aid booth at a church growth conference. I thought about it but said no because a few weeks earlier I had gone to a fair and after walking for 10 or 15 minutes I could no longer stand. I had to go to the car and wait until everyone else was ready to leave. Just the hour long car ride to the venue would leave me in pain not to mention the hours spent at the conference. I knew that by the time I'd get home I would not be able to move.*
>
> *I was in constant pain and it took great effort to be able to do anything. At that point I cried out to the Lord, "You said the harvest is plentiful and the laborers are few. Lord I am willing to be a laborer, but I cannot work in this condition."*

"Please take away the pain."

In 1994 my family and I were in a car accident and I

had a whiplash injury. Within two hours of the accident I suffered neck pain and three months later there came a day when I could not move and had to be hospitalized. A month later I had lower back surgery—lumbar laminectomies and discectomy and three months later neck surgery—cervical laminectomies for herniated discs.

The surgeries solved the extended pains along my arms and legs but the ones in my neck and lower back persisted. Lifting my hands, leaning forward, and getting out of bed were painful experiences and I thanked God for each day that I could stand.

I was a nurse at San Fernando General Hospital and the sick leave continued for 16 months. Everyone kept telling me to go back to work, and I did for one year. During this time, despite the efforts of the administration to give me "light duties," I went to work each day in constant pain and came home with even more. The cycle continued.

I took pain killers, muscle relaxants, and antidepressants every day just to be able to make it. My feet began swelling and my doctor advised against taking the medication all the time since it could cause liver and kidney damage and would not be detected until it was too late. So I began taking the medications only when absolutely necessary. Emotionally I was not coping well and it eventually led to me retiring on medical grounds at the age of 38.

"THE HEALING IS COMING"

After my retirement from nursing, my family and I

found a Spirit-filled church that preached the unadulterated Word of God. This began a work of prospering my soul.

Physically, however, there were many challenges. The pain and numbness in my arms and legs were increasing. At times, things would fall out of my hands and walking was getting to be a difficult task.

After I had done everything possible in my own strength, I decided to turn it all over to God.

The Lord woke me out of my sleep on the night of August, 15, 2002. I was not dreaming. I was wide awake and four words were impressed on my heart: "The healing is coming."

I started giving God thanks, thinking He was going to use a medication I had begun to take two days earlier to heal me.

In the days following what the Lord had told me, I shared my experience with only three friends. The last one I told was a nurse who asked me in the car park after church: "Are you having a hard time today?"

I was in a lot of pain, but shared with her the deep feeling in my heart and commented, "I don't know how, when, or where, but I know 'the healing is coming.'"

Little did I know it was only hours away.

TYPICAL EXCUSES

That Sunday night I went to a prayer service we had

before the evening service. We prayed for God to work signs and wonders in the meetings that would be held on the Monday and Tuesday nights by a woman named Joan Gieson, who had worked with Kathryn Kuhlman and Benny Hinn.

As I made my way down the stairs to the sanctuary, I had to hold tightly onto the rail and take each step carefully. The pain was intense and each step was a big effort.

Even though the meetings were scheduled Monday and Tuesday, the pastor had arranged for Joan Gieson to be introduced to the congregation on that Sunday evening.

Halfway through the service, Mrs. Gieson was brought to the platform and she spoke for a few minutes. I remember her saying, "I've been all around the world, but I've never been to a church where there were so many men."

I was a little embarrassed. My husband and youngest boy had gone to pick up our two teenage sons who had spent the weekend at a camp. Actually, my husband and I had been experiencing marital difficulties.

When I returned home, I told my boys I wanted them to go to the healing and deliverance services with me, but they made typical excuses, wanting to play football instead.

On Monday, my husband had forgotten about the service, so I went by myself.

"YOU ARE IN THE RIGHT PLACE"

As I was driving to church, I prayed, "Lord, if you

heal me tonight my boys and husband will not be there to see it, but it's okay."

When I arrived—more than an hour ahead of time—someone asked me, "Why are you here so early?" I answered, "If I knew there would be food here and I was hungry, wouldn't I be early?"

There were only three other people in the sanctuary at the time. One gentleman, John, I knew from my childhood. He asked about my nursing and I told him I didn't work anymore because of my back. "Well, you are in the right place," he answered.

As the singing and worship began, the church started to fill up. Suddenly my eldest son came in and was standing beside me. Tears started pouring from my eyes and I told him, "Thank you so much for being here. You don't know what this means to me." Before long, my other two sons and my husband slipped into the row.

"NO MORE PAIN"

The service was handed over to Joan Gieson and she began calling out conditions of deafness and blindness. Then she said, "There's one who has been in an accident with a partial paralysis." I said in my heart, "Lord, she's not saying it right. I'm not paralyzed" (not remembering the day I couldn't move).

She took some time with the deaf people and they were miraculously healed. Then she called for the one who had been in the car accident and hurt their back. I said "Lord, she's saying it right this time" and quickly put my hand up to be seen.

I was escorted by one of the workers to the platform where I was prayed for, stretched over the dear lady's back and then made to do what I couldn't do before.

I thought "It was not about what I couldn't do, since I could do everything but just with pain." I decided to try straight leg raises since I couldn't do them without extreme discomfort. At first it really hurt and the woman prayed "No more pain" — and encouraged me to try it again and again.

I now felt a new pain, not the one I was accustomed to. I was feeling it in the bundle of muscles at the front of my leg. Mrs. Gieson commented that this was because I had not used those muscles for a long time. I was soon making a full 90 degree angle without the nerve pain.

Before a packed church, the Lord had performed a miracle of healing in my body. After that everything was a bit dazed to me. I really did not hear or remember what was said and only know now because I listened to the tapes of the service afterwards.

THE GREAT PHYSICIAN

Mrs. Gieson began her message then turned her attention to me again and called for my husband and children to come forward. She had me run and then insisted I give my husband a kiss.

My nine-year-old son told the congregation he was "very happy" about my healing since he was not able to play with me for any long periods of time. The people were deeply moved and it dispelled any doubt of the healing. My family knew exactly what I had gone through. Praise God!

That night I received five miracles:

1. My children being present for the service.
2. A physical healing.
3. A restored marriage—the kiss was part of the process.
4. The work the Lord was doing in our children's lives.
5. A new boldness I received to declare the Gospel.

I have known pain and understand the human effort involved in the attempt to make me well. Far more important, however, I have experienced the miraculous touch of our Lord Jesus, the Great Physician, the Mighty Healer. There is no comparison.

Put your trust in the Lord. He is the Healer. We just have to WAIT ON THE LORD.

A Final Word

Today, as you have read these accounts of God's miraculous power, you may be asking, "What about me? What do I have to do to receive a healing or deliverance?"

My friend, God sent His precious Son to die on a cross—not only for your salvation, but also for your healing. The Bible declares, *"He was wounded for our transgressions, He was bruised for our iniquities; the chastisement for our peace was upon Him, and by His stripes we are healed"* (Isaiah 53:5).

Healing and deliverance are not the result of something we personally do, they are the result of what Christ has already done.

Hallelujah for the cross!

This very moment, I am asking you to reach out in faith and claim your miracle. The words of this inspiring chorus still ring true:

> Got any rivers, you think are uncrossable?
> Got any mountains you can't tunnel through?
> God specializes in things thought impossible.
> And He will do what no other power can do.

DO YOU KNOW JESUS?

*A*llow me to me ask a personal question. Do you know this wonderful Jesus who I have talked about in every story? Well, you *can!*

Ask yourself, "Am I going to heaven?" If you are hesitant and admit, "I don't know," the Bible tells us you can be absolutely sure. When Adam and Eve disobeyed God in the Garden of Eden, sin entered into every person born in the world. Romans 3:23 says, *"For all have sinned, and come short of the glory of God"* (KJV).

So my friend, we are all sinners. And one day, when we meet our heavenly Father, somehow those sins will have to be paid for. But God in His marvelous love, sent His only Son to become sin for you and me, and to pay the price for our transgressions.

The Bible declares that unless a person is born again, he cannot enter into the kingdom of heaven (John 3:3). So how can you be born again? Simply ask Jesus to be the Lord of your heart, to forgive you, and to live and rule in your life.

Ask Him to wash you with His precious blood and cleanse all the sins you have committed. He will change you eternally. Then thank Jesus and believe He has done what you have asked.

Now open your heart and receive Christ. Begin to praise Him, because this simple confession will set you free (Romans 10:9-10).

The two of us will meet in heaven someday and I look forward to that moment. But until then please begin to read your Bible every day, and start forgiving everyone who has sinned against you. You no longer have to carry the old junk of your past around any longer, regardless of what it was. When you let go of it, you will find everlasting freedom.

Today, begin living a new chapter of your life.

I look forward to what God will do in and through you. See you in heaven! I love you.

– Joan

To Contact the Author, Please Write:

Joan Gieson Ministries of Love
P.O Box 45407
St. Louis, MO 63145

www.joangieson.com

To contact Joan Gieson's St. Louis Healing Rooms,
write to the address above or call 314-298-7771
to make an appointment.

Please contact this ministry if you would like
to volunteer or donate items for the Gieson's Annual
Christmas Outreach. We rely solely on volunteers
and donations to make this event a success.

Other products by Joan Gieson can be
found on her website.

One final note. Our publisher has asked us to compile
a book titled *Things Thought Impossible, Volume II.* It
will be comprised of stories from our readers. If you have
a documented account of how God has performed a miracle
in your life, or in the life of someone you love, please send it
to me in approximately 800 to 1,000 words. Mail it to the
above address along with a note giving us permission
to include it if the publisher so chooses.